Building Business Capacity

Building Business Capacity

How Continuous Improvement Yields Exponential Growth

Sheryl Hardin

BUSINESS EXPERT PRESS

Leader in applied, concise business books

Building Business Capacity:
How Continuous Improvement Yields Exponential Growth

Cover design by Keisha Whaley

Interior design by Exeter Premedia Services Private Ltd., Chennai, India

First published in 2022 by
Business Expert Press, LLC
222 East 46th Street, New York, NY 10017
www.businessexpertpress.com

ISBN-13: 978-1-63742-267-0 (hardback)
ISBN-13: 978-1-63742-266-3 (paperback)
ISBN-13: 978-1-63742-268-7 (e-book)

Business Expert Press Entrepreneurship and Small Business
Management Collection

First edition: 2022

10 9 8 7 6 5 4 3 2 1

Dedicated to CEO of O'Neill Enterprises, Lin O'Neill, without whom this book would never have been written. She gently pulled me into the world of small business telling me I was going to love these owners. She said their tenacity and resilience would inspire and motive me. She was right.

Description

Change your future for the better by growing a small business fraction by fraction.

Building Small Business Capacity provides a roadmap to help entrepreneurs achieve exponential growth through constant improvement. Learn to own your business and avoid having your business own you. Leverage proven best practices used to guide businesses for decades. Walk through useful exercises, checklists, questionnaires, forms, and templates designed to help entrepreneurs like you gain clarity into the most essential aspects of successfully doing business because you deserve success.

Too many business books talk about why to go into business. Some may even tell you what you should do once you start. However too few answer the question of how to run your business while growing capacity. As it turns out there is **a secret to success**.

Proven best practices are best practices for a reason. It does not matter if you run a 10-person business or a 10,000-person conglomerate. Adhering to best practices creates the infrastructure and environment necessary to grow capacity and be successful. *Building Small Business Capacity* allows you to take advantage of strategies and tools you can integrate into your business today to run more efficiently and effectively starting tomorrow.

Keywords

best book to increase business capacity; roadmap to success exponential growth and prosperity; useful business templates checklists and forms free; how entrepreneurs know when an opportunity is right; business growth with constant process improvement; competitive advantage using strategic management; getting your business unstuck to grow

Contents

Introduction xi

Chapter 1   Growing Capacity With Constant Improvement 1
Chapter 2   Who 5
Chapter 3   Why 15
Chapter 4   What 25
Chapter 5   How 27
Chapter 6   Cycles 51
Chapter 7   Where 153
Chapter 8   Change 159
Chapter 9   Maintain 207

Position List 233
Accelerators 239
Ancillaries 241
References 243
About the Author 249
Index 251

Introduction

Building Business Capacity is a roadmap to help you achieve exponential growth by helping you and/or your leadership team gain clarity into the most essential aspects of business. It is about operating a business using best practices and constant process improvement to help ensure success.

All businesses, large or small, are run by a set of business practices. Consciously or unconsciously, those practices govern day-to-day policies, procedures, and workflows. They become the backdrop to decision making throughout the company. These practices do in fact create the systems used to operate any business of any size.

The book is laid out in a series of essays to make reading easier. Sections are brief but packed with useful information and steps that can be implemented right away. In the first part of the book, readers are asked to define who the business is and why it exists. If you do not own a business yet, it can be helpful to imagine a business you might own one day. Going through the chapters and the exercises with a business in mind makes the information more easily digestible.

Some readers may find it helpful to read the book all the way through. Others may want to read and use each section over time as they build a new business or make changes to one that already exists. Defining Who, Why, What, Where, and How helps educate owners about their own business in ways many find surprising. Where becomes obvious.

People have been doing business for thousands of years. Over the last 100 years, business practices have been widely studied. These studies help provide a systemic roadmap to success. Take this opportunity to take a systemic look at your own business as a group of systems that create an operation that either helps or hinders you in staying on the right track.

What is meant by group of systems? Each business, whether run by a single owner or a leadership team, has a diverse set of operations. These must work smoothly covering all the functions a business must do to successfully make a profit. There are the systems for accounting, marketing and selling, creating your goods or services, and so on. Systems are simply a set of processes used routinely to get some function of your business done on a regular basis.

These systems happen organically over time if no thought is given to your operations. The problem with that is that organic systems are rarely consistent. Organic systems are habits. Habits may include processes that actually harm your business.

Capacity gives entrepreneurs and leadership teams key tactics to build healthy habits allowing for the flexibility to change for the better when necessary. These best practices are more likely to contribute to the ultimate goals of the business. Using the tools, you learn to better manage, change, and grow. You create a better foundation on which to build capacity.

CHAPTER 1

Growing Capacity With Constant Improvement

Small businesses are a force in the United States providing 60.6 million people with jobs according to a 2020 Small Business Administration (SBA) study. The capacity of small businesses to grow directly impacts the capacity of the economy to grow. But what is capacity? When a group of executives were asked how to define capacity, Sales Director at VEM Tooling David Reid, responded, "The term 'Capacity' in the field of business can be defined as the facility or power to produce, perform, or deploy." (Reid 2021) Simply put, capacity is the ability to increase sales and work volume by getting things done faster and/or better than before. When done correctly more work means more revenue.

Businesses that focus on building capacity by consistently improving systems supporting a better use of resources including people and technology become more effective and efficient. This supports good decision making, which in turn supports success. Regardless of whether your business is a three person operation or a 33,000 person enterprise, when each system supports all the other systems, the business grows capacity. The 2021 Deloitte Global Human Capital Trends survey (Figure 1.1) reported that "building workforce capability" was number two in a list of actions important to executives considering workforce transformations. The first was celebrating "growth, adaptability, and resilience" which are after all indicators of a business's ability to grow capacity. (Deloitte Global Human Capital 2021).

Building capacity requires effort. It may take time before you see results. Consider these questions before committing:

- If you could do something that would likely make your business more valuable, would you do that?

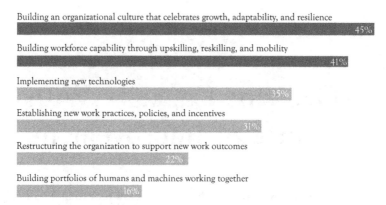

Building an organizational culture that celebrates growth, adaptability, and resilience
45%

Building workforce capability through upskilling, reskilling, and mobility
41%

Implementing new technologies
35%

Establishing new work practices, policies, and incentives
31%

Restructuring the organization to support new work outcomes
22%

Building portfolios of humans and machines working together
16%

Figure 1.1 Deloitte Global Human Capital Trends survey transforming work

Note: n=3,630 (executives)

- If you could build an organization from the ground up that is more likely to succeed, would you do that?
- What if you had to work for six months or a year to make your business 15 to 25 percent more valuable? Would *that* investment be worth your time?

What are the most important actions you are taking or will take to transform work?

Who, Why, What, How, and Where

It does not matter if you are considering starting a business, you are a current startup, or you have been in business for a long time. These questions open the door to examine or plan for the processes that make a business run efficiently and effectively. A solo entrepreneur needs to understand business as much as a company with a leadership team of an international company.

Try not to skip around as you read. Sometimes business owners and leaders find that the section they had the least interest in is the section where they need to do the most work. Lack of interest does not equate to lack of need.

There is a process that can be followed for everything. A business is an entity with a reputation or a reputation about to be built. Your journey begins by defining who your business is today. Who you work for is one of the first things you tell people when they ask what you do.

The journey continues by asking why. Why take on a new business or a new business opportunity? Why is the inspiration. Owning your own business requires a lot of energy. Building your business fraction by fraction, one opportunity at a time, requires dedication. Inspiration provides the energy to move toward the possibilities of the future. Inspiration carries you through to your end goal even when things get hard.

What you do is based on an opportunity to serve the needs of your customers. Carefully looking at how your current or your next opportunity serves those needs offers a more accurate vision for the future of your company. One that will lead you to success in a shorter timeframe.

How you get where you want to go with your business is the single biggest factor in how long it takes you to reach success. Have you ever looked at your competitors and wondered why they are more or maybe even less successful than you? It very often comes down to how they do what they do. When you think past survival and begin concentrating on long-term growth and new business opportunities you build the capacity for success. Your goals become clearer.

As you expand capacity, you must reconsider where you do business. The more you understand your business, the better prepared you are to determine where you should operate in the future. Are you best served by a virtual workforce, single or multiple locations, brick and mortar stores, and/or an online storefront? Is there a combination of choices that works best for you? Where becomes more obvious.

CHAPTER 2

Who

Genius gives birth, talent delivers.

—Jack Kerouac

Before your customers can buy your products or services, they must know that your company exists. You must teach them in person, on paper, or online who your company is and why they should care about it. Before you do, you must understand yourself.

Start by answering these questions:

- What do you have to offer?
- Why you are unique?
- Does what you have to offer meets their needs?
- Is your business trustworthy?

The first three questions tend to be easier to answer than the last. These factors impact the answer:

- History
- Reputation
- Culture

History

Every business has a story. It begins with the inspiration and ends with wherever you are today. In-between, the beginning and today is the story of how you got here. Financing or investment may hinge on how well you tell the story of your history both verbally and in writing. Write out a brief history. Create a compelling and inspiring story by answering these questions.

Paragraph One

- How did the idea to start this business come to you?
- What is your experience and what skills did you have that prepared you for this journey?
- What inspires you to keep going?
- How have your team members impacted your journey with their expertise and skills?

Paragraph Two

- What three key important things have happened on your journey as a business owner?

Paragraph Three

- Where did, or where will, you get the funds from to start the business?
- How many people do you employ including contractors and temporary workers?
- How much have you and any partners invested in the business?

Existing Business Only

- What was your beginning revenue and what is your revenue today?

Reputation

Your business reputation is a key factor in your creditability. Your own reputation matters as well. You are not as insulated from your business as leaders of corporations often are. You and your team represent your business wherever you are and whatever you are doing or saying in public. This includes on social media.

Cultivate a good reputation by:

- Treating your customers well
- Negotiating fairly

- Paying on time
- Meeting deadlines
- Upholding your end of contracts
- Being professional
- Remembering you are always a representative of your company on and off the clock

Complete the following Reputation Checklist (Figure 2.1) to begin to understand your business reputation. If are a startup or are considering a startup, answer the questions from the perspective of your personal reputation. Put a check in each box if you agree with the statement. Put an X in those boxes where you do not agree with the statement.

Reputation Checklist

	Bills are paid on time and creditors are happy.
	The business has a website, a business phone, and a business e-mail establishing credibility.
	Online reviews from customers are positive and get four or more stars on 90 percent of all reviews.
	Others are willing to offer testimonials in favor of your business and your work. (If you do not know the answer, ask 10 customers / people to write a brief one-to-three sentence recommendation and see what they return to you.)
	Reviews for your business are as good as your top three competitors or better.
	Social media posts written by you or your employees are in good taste and show respect for others.
	There are no stories in print or online that depict you personally or your employees in a bad light such as partying, fights, arrests, displays of offensive gestures, controversial comments, or bias or insensitive comments toward others.
	Some or all of new work or purchases come from referrals or recommendations.
	Details about business awards, certifications, badges, and press can easily be found.
	You have a customer/contact list of people you market to who are fans.
	Your business is listed on Dunn and Bradstreet and maintains a favorable rating.
	Your business is listed on the Better Business Bureau (BBB) and maintains a favorable rating.
	You do not have any outstanding legal judgments against you.
	You do not have any negative press about your product, services, or business activities.
	You are known for being a collaborative negotiator.

Figure 2.1 Reputation Checklist

Review your answers and work quickly to correct any issues that you see.

Reforming Your Reputation

Reputations can be damaged for a number of reasons. Many entrepreneurs start businesses as a way out of bad circumstances and so must deal with reputation issues immediately. Unemployment, inferior credit, or poor reputation sometimes makes creating your own job the best next step. Other entrepreneurs get into trouble along the way while learning the art of running a business.

If your reputation review indicated that yours could use a tune up, start now. Your new reputation begins today. Help is available for these common issues:

- Financial trouble
- Bad online reviews
- Disruptions in service
- Poor delivery
- Legal issues
- Tough negotiations

Financial Trouble

Financial issues often plague small businesses at some point. The SBA, Small Business Development Council (SBDC), Minority Supplier Development Council (MSDC), and a host of other state and local organizations exist to assist motivated individuals wanting a better life for themselves through business ownership. They can help you sort out financial issues. Colleges often provide support as well through free programs designed to give their accounting students real experience. Some accelerators such as Business Owner's MBA (BOMBA) focus on teaching business owners best financial business practices. Seek out advice and get support.

Bad Online Reviews

Poor reviews hurt companies that provide services as well as those who offer products. If your company has a BBB or Dunn and Bradstreet (D and B) rating that is poor, work to resolve the issues or differences with your customers who are unhappy as quickly as possible. If you have a bad online review, address it immediately by apologizing even if you are not wrong. Reply to your customer that you are sorry because they are unhappy without admitting any guilt. Respond with kind words. Never argue. Offer a solution if possible so that potential customers see that you care.

Disruptions in Service

Disruptions can be caused by a number of factors, some of which may be out of your control. Things happen as we saw throughout 2020 and 2021. Extreme weather and a global supply chain broken first by tariff battles and then by the Covid-19 pandemic caused challenges. Customers may not be happy but most often they understand when things happen you cannot control.

As soon as you know about a problem, inform everyone about to be impacted. Be honest with your customers about what happened and why. Let those impacted know what you have done to correct the situation.

Poor Delivery

This is different from disruptions in service. These issues are caused by internal problems that should have been prevented. Poor delivery has to do with incidents where your products or services were not delivered or when the quality of your goods or services was not as good as your customer deserved. Make amends when possible by refunding money or redoing work at your own cost. The sooner you rectify the situation the better. Take a hard look at what went wrong and make changes so it does not happen again.

Legal Issues

Lawsuits, even frivolous lawsuits, often make your customers uneasy. Investors and bankers are likely to shy away from your business as long as a judgment is pending. If you can resolve the matter before a court case is filed, you are much better off. If you cannot then work with a good lawyer to resolve pending litigation as quickly as possible. Take care to be fair.

Tough Negotiations

Tough negotiators may be admired by some but studies show that a reputation for being a tough negotiator may hurt you in the marketplace. Catherine Tinsley PhD, executive director of Georgetown McDonough's Executive Master's in Leadership program, studied gender-based negotiation tactics. She discovered that those who had a reputation for being collaborative, faired better in negotiations than those with a reputation for being tough, or whose reputation was unknown. When women were seen as tough negotiators, they experienced more backlash than men did. This was true even if the reputation was not based on any real facts. (Tinsley PhD 2012)

> Angie Strader, former military negotiator and small business owner, had this to say, "I do not tell people I was a military-trained hostage negotiator because it puts people on the defensive. They immediately think I have an unfair advantage. Experience has taught me that to succeed in a negotiation, you have to gain people's trust by showing that you honestly and sincerely care about both sides reaching a mutually beneficial agreement.
>
> This does not mean that you have to give in to the other side's demands; it means that both sides can get to a point where they can walk away feeling like they won, or at the very least, that they didn't lose. It takes patience and compassion to bring a peaceful end to a tense situation. In a successful negotiation, everyone gets out safely, feels like they won, and is willing to come back to the table another day." (Strader 2021)

Culture

Your company culture defines your business environment. Executives who participated in the 2021 Deloitte Global Human Capital Trends survey reported that building an organization that celebrates culture, celebrates growth, is adaptable, and shows resilience was ranked as most important in building capacity through workforce transformation. Similarly, workers who participated in the study ranked "improving worker well-being" as third in their concerns. (Deloitte Global Human Capital 2021)

Your culture may be the most important driver of workforce contentment. Happy resources tend to do better work. Studies show that workers who like their jobs perform better. Economists Andrew Oswald PhD, Eugenio Proto PhD, and Daniel Sgroi PhD from the department of economics at the University of Warwick tested the idea that happy employees work harder in three different experiments. They discovered, "The treated[tested] individuals have approximately 12 percent greater productivity." (Oswald, Proto, and Sgroi 2015)

It is clear to see that company culture is important to your success. Even if you have no employees yet, answer the questions for yourself considering whether you agree or disagree with how important each statement would likely be to your future.

Culture Quiz

On a scale of 1 to 10, determine how much you agree with the statement with 1 being Disagree Strongly and 10 being Agree Strongly (see the Culture Quiz in Figure 2.2). Select the box to the right of the number that best represents what you believe to be true. Your answers will be anonymous. Please answer truthfully.

---

1. This is a company I would recommend to others looking for a job.

Disagree   Agree

1 ☐ 2 ☐ 3 ☐ 4 ☐ 5 ☐ 6 ☐ 7 ☐ 8 ☐ 9 ☐ 10 ☐

2. I know the vision of the company.

Disagree   Agree

1 ☐ 2 ☐ 3 ☐ 4 ☐ 5 ☐ 6 ☐ 7 ☐ 8 ☐ 9 ☐ 10 ☐

---

3. I know the mission of the company.

Disagree   Agree

1 ☐ 2 ☐ 3 ☐ 4 ☐ 5 ☐ 6 ☐ 7 ☐ 8 ☐ 9 ☐ 10 ☐

4. I feel empowered to make my own decisions about my work.

Disagree   Agree

1 ☐ 2 ☐ 3 ☐ 4 ☐ 5 ☐ 6 ☐ 7 ☐ 8 ☐ 9 ☐ 10 ☐

5. My ideas for improvement are heard and fairly evaluated.

Disagree   Agree

1 ☐ 2 ☐ 3 ☐ 4 ☐ 5 ☐ 6 ☐ 7 ☐ 8 ☐ 9 ☐ 10 ☐

6. The atmosphere among my co-workers is friendly.

Disagree   Agree

1 ☐ 2 ☐ 3 ☐ 4 ☐ 5 ☐ 6 ☐ 7 ☐ 8 ☐ 9 ☐ 10 ☐

7. I am treated with respect.

Disagree   Agree

1 ☐ 2 ☐ 3 ☐ 4 ☐ 5 ☐ 6 ☐ 7 ☐ 8 ☐ 9 ☐ 10 ☐

8. My concerns are taken seriously.

Disagree   Agree

1 ☐ 2 ☐ 3 ☐ 4 ☐ 5 ☐ 6 ☐ 7 ☐ 8 ☐ 9 ☐ 10 ☐

9. My job responsibilities are clear.

Disagree   Agree

1 ☐ 2 ☐ 3 ☐ 4 ☐ 5 ☐ 6 ☐ 7 ☐ 8 ☐ 9 ☐ 10 ☐

10. I understand how my performance is evaluated.

Disagree   Agree

1 ☐ 2 ☐ 3 ☐ 4 ☐ 5 ☐ 6 ☐ 7 ☐ 8 ☐ 9 ☐ 10 ☐

11. I expect to have opportunities for career growth.

Disagree   Agree

1 ☐ 2 ☐ 3 ☐ 4 ☐ 5 ☐ 6 ☐ 7 ☐ 8 ☐ 9 ☐ 10 ☐

12. I plan to stay with the company for one or more years.

Disagree   Agree

1 ☐ 2 ☐ 3 ☐ 4 ☐ 5 ☐ 6 ☐ 7 ☐ 8 ☐ 9 ☐ 10 ☐

13. I understand and believe in the company values.

Disagree   Agree

1 ☐ 2 ☐ 3 ☐ 4 ☐ 5 ☐ 6 ☐ 7 ☐ 8 ☐ 9 ☐ 10 ☐

14. I am proud to work for this company.

Disagree   Agree

1 ☐ 2 ☐ 3 ☐ 4 ☐ 5 ☐ 6 ☐ 7 ☐ 8 ☐ 9 ☐ 10 ☐

Figure 2.2 Culture Quiz

CHAPTER 3

Why

Far and away the best prize that life offers is the chance to work hard at work worth doing.

—Theodore Roosevelt

Why go into business? Why did you or why would you? The reasons may be as different as each business owner. Growing income may be the reason most often cited but certainly not the only one. Some business owners go into business to provide employment for their family, gain greater flexibility in their careers, recover from hardship, or even change the world. Understanding why helps you face the risks and remain motivated as you grow capacity.

Facing the Risks

Millions of small business owners have said "yes" to the challenge and have taken the risk. There is risk involved after all. This is true but it may not be as risky as you have been led to believe. It is commonly thought as many as 80 percent of new businesses fail in the first five years. That failure rate can be daunting. However, a closer look by experts has begun to suggest the failure rate during years not impacted by extreme events such as the 2020 Covid-19 pandemic may be much lower.

Patricia Greene, PhD, former director of the Women's Bureau of the U.S. Department of Labor, reports, "We don't really know the success rate of businesses in the United States. We hear a lot of chatter, and people often throw out the tired alliteration that four out of five fail in the first five years. The SBA does not track failures, they track continuance and discontinuance. Who is still there the next time they count and who is not there." (Greene 2021)

The U.S. Chamber of Commerce reports that 99.9 percent of all businesses in the United States are small businesses. The SBA reports that businesses with 20 to 99 employees account for most new employment each year. If it were true that the first five years of owning a business is as precarious as first thought, what would that say about the economy as a whole? Greene explains her theory as to why new businesses are more resilient than commonly believed. "There are many reasons not to be there. The business might have failed, or the owner might have retired and closed it. It might have been sold. it might have been incorporated, and therefore become a new business entity. While it's certainly not easy to grow and sustain a business, working from inaccurate data doesn't help anyone." (Greene 2021)

Finding the Motivation

Motivation is a driving force. Motivation is important because that passion keeps a small business owner from giving up when times get hard. Motivation helps push past burnout. Many times, it is the thing a struggling business owner needs to remember to avoid quitting right before success. This is the reason it is so important to understand why.

Having considered who you are as a business owner or leader and who your business is in the world, you know enough to answer the next question. Why go into business or pursue a new opportunity? Why matters.

In a 2020 survey conducted by Cox Business, 66 percent of small business owners reported they got into business to be the boss and build something of their own (Cox Business 2020). Most owners or potential owners like you choose their business because they are good at something they do. Ask yourself, why do you choose to run a business instead of being employed?

Everything we learn tomorrow begins with what we know today. You have spent a lifetime developing skills and building knowledge that has made you the business leader you are today. Assessing who you are based on everything you have learned today as a person, a leader, a business owner, and a business helps guide you on your journey to success.

Once your history is clear, and you know the foundation upon which you stand it is time to look toward the future as if you were starting today.

A very clear mission statement with a target end goal creates a straighter path to success. If you know where you are starting from and where you are headed, it is easier to create the map from point A to point B.

If you have been so busy running your business that you have not considered what success looks like, there is no better time than the present. Create and sustain a clear and accurate end goal to develop a clear and accurate vision.

Question Your Motives

Consider your motives by answering these questions.

1. Why are you an entrepreneur?
2. What do you get out of or expect that you will get out of owning your own business and being your own boss?
3. Are you actually suited to your business?
4. Why did you choose the business you are in, or are planning to start?
5. Is it the right business?

Knowing the answers helps you determine how you move forward. So, why are these tough questions sometimes? It comes back to the fact that you probably started your business based on your own best skills. Doctors, lawyers, teachers, plumbers, and construction workers often say they liked the thing they DID and they were good at it. When you delve into why you own a business and really consider the answers, some of you may find that you do not like being a business owner. However, most of you will discover you might need more information, education, or assistance to make the difficult parts of owning a business easier. You may also need a way to identify those tasks that keep you from enjoying your business so that you can hand those off and find joy again.

Assessing Motivation

You may find that in the course of growing capacity, you are bogged down in tasks you do not enjoy. Work becomes a chore. While it is unlikely that you can create work for yourself that avoids everything you dislike, thoughtful consideration may make reducing the number of tasks you avoid easier. Complete the motivational assessment exercise that follows to learn more.

Motivational Assessment

Create a two-column list. First, make a list of the things you really enjoy doing including the tasks that you rarely procrastinate about before starting. Put that list on the left side of your paper. On the right side of your paper, make a list of all the things you have to do for your business that you are likely to put off doing.

Table 3.1 Motivational Assessment Template

Like	Procrastinate
Calling on Clients	Accounting
Networking	Creating work schedules

When you are done look at the list (Table 3.1). You may find there are things on the Procrastinate side that you actually thought you liked to do. You may also be surprised by the number of tasks on the "Like" side of the paper you did not expect. As you grow capacity, you want to hand over the tasks you do not enjoy to your team members. Your Procrastinate list should grow shorter and shorter.

Starting Today

Consider looking at your business as if you were starting today. Do this even if you have been operating your business for some time. Looking at your operations with fresh eyes assists you in seeing things you may otherwise miss. If you are considering starting a business, then looking at what it would look like if you started today helps as well. Even if you are operating a fairly new startup organization, looking at your business as if you were just starting it today provides you with a perspective that offers options you might not otherwise see.

Begin by defining or redefining your business. Start with the values that make you proud to own your business. Given that your values must align with all that you do, define your company's mission. When you understand your mission, define your exit strategy or your end goal. Understanding both your mission and your exit strategy leads you to your vision for your business going forward.

Company Values

Values are core beliefs. Capacity-driven businesses operate from four to six core values that form a value statement. A value statement is a belief that you as a business owner expect all members of your organization to live by collectively. These are the boundaries used when making business decisions. These beliefs drive leadership behavior acting as a filter whenever you make key decisions.

They include but are not limited to thoughts like the following:

- We operate with integrity.
- Our organization believes in the value of diversity and respects differences.
- We value transparency and actively work to be open and honest with our team members and our customers.
- We believe that our work must beneficially impact all those with whom we come into contact.
- We provide a place of connection.

Mission

Mission statements are tricky things. Oftentimes, a mission statement is seen as a collection of meaningless pretty words. The purpose of a mission statement is to excite you as a business owner about what it is you are planning to achieve. There are just a few simple steps to crafting a mission statement that inspires you and your team, like the following examples:

Mission Examples

Here are three examples of clear concise and compelling mission statements.

- **Asana**
  To help humanity thrive by enabling all teams to work together effortlessly. (Moskovitz 2021)
- **Starbucks**
  To inspire and nurture the human spirit—one person, one cup, and one neighborhood at a time. (Starbucks 2021)
- **CapacitySquared (C2)**
  Create a world-class member organization of small business owners, the entities they serve, and the key people who serve them so that each one has the opportunity to grow to their highest capacity. (Hardin 2021)

Crafting Your Mission Statement

Follow the ensuing steps to create a meaningful mission statement:

Step One—Prepare to Brainstorm

Have every member of your leadership team answer the following questions:

1. What made you want to start/lead this company?
2. When people are asked about your company what do you want them to say?
3. What sets you apart, or what would you like to set you apart from your competition?
4. If you did not need money, what about your company would motivate you to get up and come into work each day?
5. Why do you think others might want to join your company?

Step Two—Brainstorm

1. Compare the answers as a group writing each where they can be seen.
2. Review the list taking notice of any similarities.

3. Ask your team members which items they agree with one-by-one noting the total for each.

4. Ask your team members which items inspire them going over each one-by-one noting the total for each.

5. Based on what you know now, ask each team member to answer these three questions.
   - What does your company do?
   - What is your ultimate goal?
   - What is most important to you?

6. Compare your answers.

Step Three—Write Your Statement

1. Write a one-to-three sentence statement together as a team that covers the same questions.
   - What does your company do?
   - What is your ultimate goal?
   - What is most important to you?

2. Ask yourself if looking at your mission statement compels you to move forward and makes you smile. If not, keep working on your wording until it does.

3. Display your final version in some way that makes it easy for your entire company to see.

Determining Your End Goal

Your end goal is your exit strategy, not your mission-driven ultimate goal. Your exit strategy is how you plan to leave your business one day. No matter what you are in planning for or how far away your exit might be, know your strategy. Beginning today with the end in mind helps keep you on target.

Review the following strategies to see which one best matches your current needs:

- Passive ownership that continues by
  ○ Allowing one or more family members or partners to inherit your ongoing enterprise;

- Transferring your business to one or more family members or partners while retaining a percentage of the profits;
- Leasing your business to an operator while still retaining ownership;
- Pursuing an Initial Public Offering (IPO) that allows a board of directors to run your company while you maintain some stock ownership;
- Creating a stock ownership plan that allows you to maintain some stock while your employees run the business and hold the majority share;
- Offering a franchise to business operators while having a board run your central office so that you maintain passive ownership.

- Selling your business
  - To another company or business owner;
  - Through an employee stock ownership plan that allows your employees to gradually buy the entire business;
  - To a trusted employee;
  - By selling your percentage of ownership to your partner(s);
  - By transferring your business to one or more family members or partners without retaining any percentage of the profits;
  - By selling your assets.

If you find yourself resistant to considering your exit strategy because you do not want to be locked in, remember like everything else in your life your strategy is flexible. You may find your end game changes as your capacity grows. Nothing is carved in stone.

The one strategy to avoid is bankruptcy. All your hard work and efforts should not go into a business that will leave you heartbroken and in debt. By planning early with a strategy that focuses on what success means to you, you are less likely to shudder your doors literally or virtually.

Consider looking at your exit strategy at least once a year and taking time to decide whether to revise your end goal. Keep your end goal accurate so that everything you do can be measured against whether you are moving closer to where you want to end up. When your business decisions are driven by your mission and take you closer to a successful exit strategy no matter how far away your exit may be, you are much more likely to get there.

Vision

Vision statements, must excite you and compel you forward. Vision statements are often just a set of pretty words on a piece of paper, or a plaque, or your website just like many mission statements. Pretty words are not useful. Be bold. Your statement should be the reason you get up and go to work in the morning. Here are some good examples.

Vision Examples

Here are three examples of clear concise and compelling vision statements.

- **Nike**
  Nike exists to bring inspiration and innovation to every athlete*
  in the world.
  (*If you have a body, you are an athlete.) (Nike 2021)
- **CapacitySquared (C2)**
  Create the quintessential space where small business leaders access essential resources while building business through entrepreneurial community connections that end owner isolation and breed success fraction-by-fraction. (Capacity Squared 2021)
- **Tesla**
  Tesla's mission is to accelerate the world's transition to sustainable energy (Tesla 2021)

Creating Your Vision Statement

Create a vision statement using the following steps:

1. Ask each member of your leadership team to take a moment and consider what success looks and then answer these questions:
2. What problem do we solve for our customers?

3. Compare your answers.

4. Ask each member of your leadership team to take a moment and consider what they know now to answer these additional questions:

   (a) When all of your goals for your business have been achieved what is the one thing you would want people to say when they look back at your success?

   (b) How will things be different?

5. Compare your answers.

6. Write a one-sentence statement together.

This is your vision. It should not just make you smile, but it should be the guiding force for each step you take as you move forward. It should be a statement that you clearly use to determine if you are on or off target. Your vision is your inspiration. It is the "why" behind all that you do. Understanding it can be the difference between giving up or overcoming, should times get tough.

Understanding the Reason Behind It All

At the turn of the century, experts used to say to follow your passion and the money will come. This turned out to be bad advice. Many entrepreneurs started businesses that led them straight into bankruptcy. The hard truth is there are a lot of good business ideas that should never be done. The key reason to go into business is to be able to accomplish your mission and vision so that eventually you arrive at your end goal.

CHAPTER 4

What

Put a grain of boldness into everything you do.
—Baltazar Gracian y Morales, S.J.

What do you do? It is one of the first questions asked when you meet someone new. You must be able to answer that question when anyone asks about your business. Be ready with a quick and confident answer when asked.

Growing Capacity Through Opportunities

Moving forward with anything new is bold. Growing your capacity often means expanding and creating new opportunities for growth. Opportunities are just new business ideas you have not considered before now. Most small companies start with a limited number of products or services. Service companies often soon find they need to offer additional services because the most valuable contracts tend to go to "full service" vendors. Product companies realize they can add complementary products to make their customers happy and increase sales. Sometimes companies that sell a product find that they can grow their bottom line by offering services to implement, install, and maintain those same products. Service companies may discover that selling one or more of the products they service adds to their profit margin as well.

Opportunities are the seeds of your ideas that when properly nurtured sprout into success. Whether you are an entrepreneur considering a new business opportunity or an existing business owner contemplating expanding with another opportunity, an organized and thoughtful approach reduces risks and helps ensure success. Deciding what opportunity is right for your organization begins with fully identifying and vetting an idea.

Defining the Opportunity

Every opportunity solves a problem by meeting a need caused by a point of pain or inconvenience. Consider for example a need to keep an entire community safe by manufacturing the best customized parts necessary to ensure the reliability of a dam to avoid the pain of a dangerous flood. Perhaps you want to provide better housing for low-income single mothers to reduce the pain of substandard housing. On the other hand, the need may be to experience the pleasure of taking a bite out of a delectable dessert so good that just thinking of it makes your customer's mouth water.

It is clear to see we have many perceived needs; some are more urgent than others are. All needs present opportunities. The viability of your opportunity depends on meeting a need in your market that can be clearly stated. It may be as simple as overcoming boredom or as complicated as creating scientific breakthroughs in answer to a world problem.

Finding Your Market

Your customers may be buyers, donors, funders, service recipients, or some combination depending on whether you are for profit or nonprofit. Determining if a customer market exists is different from creating a market strategy or developing a marketing or sales plan. At this point, understanding where your opportunity fits into the marketplace determines if what you have to offer is worth pursuing. If not, you may need to consider the changes necessary to make your opportunity viable. Better to know now. The market determines what you sell. A perfect market consists of a large customer base with no reasons why you cannot reach those customers who are willing and able to pay the price you ask.

Ask yourself these questions:

1. Is there a place in the market for my opportunity now or will I have to educate customers so that they understand the need?
2. What credible data exists from reliable sources such as the U.S. Chamber of Commerce, U.S. Census, SBA, U.S. Labor Bureau, trade associations, and industry research?
3. After reviewing reliable data sources ask yourself, is my estimated market big enough to be successful?

CHAPTER 5

How

There's no shortage of remarkable ideas; what's missing is the will to execute them.

—Seth Godin

When the idea becomes an opportunity for success, it is time to move carefully. Successful entrepreneurs move at just the right speed. Avoid being impulsive by taking time to go through each step. Move forward without procrastination. Remember that following an organized and systemic approach reduces risk and helps ensure success.

Evaluating Operational Readiness

Being good at what you do does not always translate into understanding all of the factors involved in running a business. You do not have to start by knowing all the answers. Most entrepreneurs do not. Evaluate what you know about your business using an Operational Assessment.

Operational Assessments contain a list of questions about how your business is or will be run. Obviously, if you are starting a new business, you are likely to have many more gaps than someone who has been in business for a while. However, these assessments help identify gaps in businesses of any age. There are a wide variety of assessment questionnaires available. Some are longer than others are. Assessments range from two pages to a hundred pages depending on the size and complexity of the company being assessed.

Use the six page assessment audit found in resources at CapacitySquared .net to begin your assessment. Do the assessment with your leadership team if you have one because your team members may have answers you do not. If you come to a question that is not applicable, then put "N/A." If you come to a question that you do not know the answer to yet, enter

"I/We do not know yet." Add questions and thoughts the questionnaire raises in the notes section and address those as well.

Review your assessment when completed making note of your gaps. As you move forward, many of these gaps will likely be addressed. Keep your assessment handy updating it as you learn more while moving onward with your business opportunity. You may want to go over your completed assessment with a trusted adviser, leadership peer group, and/ or mentor to gain new insights. Many find reviewing the assessment with others is just as valuable as completing it.

Organization Strategic Planning

Operations is simply put everything you do to run your business. Your organization strategy sets the direction and priorities for your business creating a healthy environment for good decision making. Having a strategy often makes the difference when it comes to growing capacity without chaos and turmoil. Companies that work from a strategic plan often save time and money while avoiding frustration.

Small business owners who intentionally and carefully manage their businesses tend to do better than those who do not according to a 2017 study. After looking at 31 empirical studies, researchers Bert George, Richard Walker, and Joost Monster concluded,

> "The findings suggest that strategic planning should be part of the standard managerial approaches in contemporary organizations and contradict many of the critiques of strategic planning. The formality of the strategic planning processes (i.e., the extent to which strategic planning includes internal and external analyses and the formulation of goals, strategies, and plans) is important to enhancing organizational performance." (George, Walker, and Monster 2019)

Your operations must always strategically support your mission, vision, and values and be in alignment with your end goal. Small businesses that operate from core values inspired by the mission and vision that drive the business operate with more clarity. Grow capacity by slowly implementing the tools necessary to support your strategic direction and priorities.

Strategically run organizations utilize these tools:

- Key Performance Indicators (KPIs)
- Roadmaps to Success
- Milestone Checkpoints
- Predictable Planning Reviews
- Management Planning
- Agile Status Meetings

KPIs

KPIs measure how well you, your teams, and/or your business achieve your objectives such as reducing errors by 30 percent or increasing revenues by 15 percent. KPI metrics help mobilize your workforce and inspire success. Metrics create targets that clearly define what success looks like.

Roadmap to Success

What entrepreneurs report needing most often is a plan that they can see visually that is flexible and easy to manage. Roadmaps work well because a properly built roadmap holds all your ideas until you are ready to focus on them. Great ideas never get lost. Roadmaps help ensure your ability to grow capacity in an organized manner. Use roadmaps to decide what to focus on now so that you and your team are not fragmented, overloaded, or distracted.

Your roadmap can be built in less than a day most of the time using no technology. This does not mean that technology cannot be used. There are a myriad of software tools available to build and manage your roadmap. The steps are exactly the same with or without technology.

Building a Strategic Roadmap

Do this exercise alone or with your team members. Including your team in your Roadmap to Success is a good idea. Your team members may add valuable insights into goals and priorities otherwise missed. Use post-it notes to capture goals and move them from the roadmap to quarterly goals and then to assignments when everyone is in the same room if you are doing the exercise manually. Use any software that allows you to cut and paste shapes if you are doing the exercise online.

Step 1—Brainstorm

1. Gather your team together.
2. Make a list of issues that need resolving to consider including in your goals.
3. Create a list of possible goals for the next 12-months with no judgment.
   Note: Your goals can be simple such as:
   • Check budget estimates against actual totals every quarter.
   • Post to social media once per day.
4. Add to the list using these prompts:
   • Build sales
   • Market better
   • Improve client/customer satisfaction
   • Resolve issues
   • Be more efficient
   • Be more effective

Step 2—Prioritize and Estimate

1. Prioritize the list of goals from your brainstorming session by marking them Must Do, Want to Do, Nice to Do, and Might Never with Must Do being your highest priority.
   • Must do to survive
   • Want to do to be more efficient and/or effective
   • Nice to do to if I/we can get to it
   • Might never do because it is not a high priority
2. Estimate the amount of time it might take you to accomplish each goal in days or hours and write the estimate beside each goal.

3. Review the times and break down anything that would take more than three months into 90 day segments such as making one social media post every day for 90 days listed four times.
4. Review the list to make sure all of your goals are included, have time estimates, and have the proper priorities.

Step 3—Build the Plan

1. Create four columns so that you have one for each quarter of the year.
2. Name each column 1, 2, 3, and 4 again one for each quarter of the year (Figure 5.1).

1	2	3	4

Figure 5.1 Roadmap to Success quarterly goals

3. Add a new horizontal row and name it Unassigned.
4. Separate your Must Have goals by priority in the quarterly time slots (Figure 5.1) available based on when you want to accomplish the goal.

1	2	3	4
Unassigned			
Goal Goal Goal	Goal Goal Goal	Goal Goal Goal	Goal Goal Goal
Goal Goal Goal	Goal Goal Goal	Goal Goal Goal	Goal Goal Goal
Goal Goal Goal	Goal Goal Goal	Goal Goal Goal	Goal Goal Goal

Figure 5.2 Roadmap to Success quarterly goals

5. Add an additional horizontal row for each team member who may be put in charge of a goal.
6. Assign team members first quarter goals by moving them from Unassigned to the team member in charge (Figure 5.2).

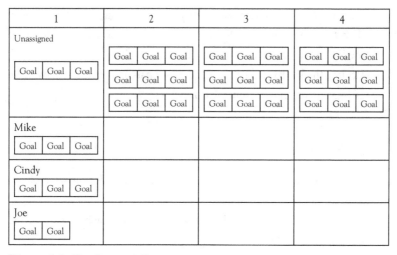

Figure 5.3 Roadmap to Success resources

Step 4—Fill the Quarter

1. Review your list and consider the time available to each resource after regular assignments are complete.
2. Remove goals from anyone who appears overloaded and put each of those back in Unassigned.
3. Give additional goal assignments to anyone who appears to have the time and skills necessary to be successful even if the goal is a lower priority so that no time is wasted.
4. Move any first quarter goals that remain unassigned to the next quarter (Figure 5.3).

Step 5—Finish the Plan

1. Repeat the process for each quarter.
2. Continue until all the goals you and your team can manage for the year are on your board and are assigned to a team member.
3. Review the board one more time to make sure the goals are achievable in the time your plan suggests. If not break the task down into timeframes for each quarter.
4. Save your work in a way that it will not be lost.

5. Review the items that remain unassigned on your roadmap.
   Note: These items remain on the roadmap so that the ideas are not lost. These goals may be assigned to resources if they find they have additional time. They may also be completed by added resources as they come on board. You may even wait until sometime in the future to address many of the unassigned items.

6. Continue using the roadmap to capture new goals or to reassign goals if priorities shift.

Milestone Checkpoints

Milestones are just key points where you stop for review making sure you are still on the right path. Every plan that is carried out in your business for more than three months should have milestone checkpoints. Milestones are useful at the strategic level, the business opportunity level, and the project level. Use these moments as a time to review where you are and at key decisions necessary to move forward.

For any plan to work, you need to know if you are on target. Use milestones to mark checkpoints on your plan schedule. These checkpoints measure metrics such as percentage of completion, revenue growth, customer growth, profit margin, and so on. Long-term strategic plans may require many checkpoints.

Understanding whether you are moving forward as you planned helps to determine whether the plan is working. Milestones provide moments of reflection that help you make adjustments while keeping the end goal in sight. If you do not know whether you are ahead or behind, then you cannot do course corrections. Course corrections are often necessary because the reality of working your plan can be different than you thought it would be in theory. In addition, things change as time goes. Good plans change as well.

Predictable Planning Reviews

Accurately predicting how long it takes to get things done may take some time and experience. This is one of the reasons for writing down plans and promised actions so that deadlines become a part of the company's historical record. Hold yourself and your team accountable for the predictions. As you start to build a historical record, compare the amount of time you thought it would take to do a task, resolve an issue, or complete a promise against the actual time it took. Your estimates may be off at first but understanding that gives you the information to do better next time. You may soon be surprised by how accurate you become.

Management Periods

Book time for management tasks that must be accomplished in order for your business to be successful. Schedule a meeting with yourself so that others do not book the time you need. These are meetings you make with yourself to get your work done so that working on your business does not start at 5:00 PM when everyone else is finishing up for the day. These self-appointed meetings do not have to be carved in stone. You certainly do not want to miss a big contract because you scheduled budget planning at the only time your client/customer can meet. However, do not make a habit of rescheduling frequently because this time is important to managing your business well.

Agile Status Meetings

Many entrepreneurs start their own businesses because they hate what they refer to as red tape. Red tape includes long business meetings. However, any business with two or more people requires that information be shared in a timely manner. Brief Agile Status Meetings are the answer. These allow you and your team(s) to do micro day/week planning that helps keep your larger plans on track.

Agile Status Meetings may happen daily or weekly depending on the pace of work. Schedule these brief meetings for 15 minutes and stick to your start and end times. Any longer and you are likely getting off track. In the meeting, team members answer the same questions about the day or week at hand.

Answer these questions:

- What did I accomplish yesterday/last week?
- What am I doing today/this week?

- What is in the way of success?
- Am I on schedule?

These status questions tell you a great deal. If the answers raise more complicated questions that must be addressed, set a time for that later. Address any delays. Keep a list of issues in the way of success and assign someone to address each making sure to set a deadline for resolution. These brief meetings avoid surprises that cost time and money.

Building Strong Teams

Now that you know you have a product or service the market will support, it is time to consider the right team to make your business a success. The best plans in the world will not succeed without the right team. Team members have the right skills to fit into your team where you need them and are a good match for your work environment.

Ross Perot, founder of Electronic Data Systems (EDS), started his business in his garage and grew it into a successful multinational corporation that was eventually purchased by General Motors. People who worked for EDS were not just expected to be a good fit for their jobs; they were expected to be a good match as well. EDS team members were considered some of the best skilled in their fields. EDS employees were comfortable working in a very formal work environment with a military style hierarchy, and extensive reporting requirements. Workers were expected to work on tight deadlines with the flexibility to quickly shift priorities when required. Candidates had to have great skills to fit and they had to be a match for the culture.

A Fit for Success

Candidates must have or be able to quickly learn the skills to do their job. It does not matter if the job requires great expertise like a doctor or an engineer or less like a person who makes pizza. The right fit looks different depending on the position. Candidates do not always have to arrive with the skills you need. Effective training assists new team members in acquiring the skills necessary to be a good fit. Others may not be a good fit if they have to be trained. Some people need to know more than you do.

For example, if you are not an accountant and you do not love numbers, you may want a bookkeeper and perhaps an accountant that can do the job you do not want to learn. Staying up all night making a mess of it yourself does nobody any good. Your accountant should not need any training. Your account should know more about accounting than you do.

A Match for Your Environment

When employees are the right match, they are happy in their job. They are not just the right fit, but they enjoy the culture, have the right authority, and the work they do interests them. They are happy to come to work each day and do not need much supervision. If you have to be involved in every aspect of your business to be successful, your team is not a good match. Well-matched employees are empowered to own and do their job without you hovering over their shoulders.

Matching avoids:

- Culture Contamination
- Irreplaceable Employees
- Single Sources of Failure
- Position Mismatches

Culture Contamination

Even among companies who are close competitors, cultures vary widely. Some businesses are more formal and regimented. Others are more casual and creative. Some resources may fit more easily in one environment than they do in the other.

For example, a consulting company whose teams often worked on site for clients was looking to add a software engineer to a remote team. The remote team had been given very little space, so traditional offices were not available and cubes were not a good idea. This is not uncommon for consulting groups who are used to working with what they are given even if it is just a conference room. This group had pulled together working desks in groups of five or six shared randomly. Team members took whatever seat was available when they came out of meetings.

A candidate who was a good fit was given a tour. He seemed concerned and kept asking where he would store his stapler. This was a red flag. Another candidate who fit the need was given the same tour. She seemed comfortable and told a story about working in a similar environment. She was a fit AND a match. She got the job.

It is important to remember though that matching culture is not a code for discrimination. Successful companies in the 21st century consider all resources regardless of race, creed, gender, or sexual orientation. Matches are matches to business environment not physical characteristics or personal lifestyle.

If your teams are too homogeneous, you may be missing out on the benefits of diversity including attracting the right candidates. According to a 2020 Glassdoor D&I (Diversity and Inclusion) Workplace Survey, "More than 3 in 4-employees and job seekers (76 percent) report a diverse workforce is an important factor when evaluating companies and job offers." (Harris Poll 2020) Even if you must mix things up a bit and your teams get a little uncomfortable during the change, having a wider array of perspectives can be GOOD for the bottom line.

In the 2020 report, Diversity Wins: How Inclusion Matters, researchers at McKinsey and Company studied hundreds of companies for six years. They saw that a few companies were adopting systematic, business-led approaches to diversity, equity, and inclusion (DEI) and named that group "Diversity Winners." They reported, "Our 2019 analysis finds that companies in the top quartile for gender diversity on executive teams were 25 percent more likely to have above-average profitability than companies in the fourth quartile—up from 21 percent in 2017 and 15 percent in 2014." (Dixon-Fyle, Hunt, Dolan, and Prince 2020)

Irreplaceable People Threat

Make a list of all the people in your organization that are irreplaceable. These are the people you think you could not do without. People you think have unique skills or knowledge, who if they left your company you would hurt. This includes you. Make a contingency plan for each position.

Single Source of Failure Threat

These are people who do a job that no one else does. They do it well. They may or may not be considered irreplaceable. However, if these resources were gone, there would be no one else to do their job and that would cause some pain. They may do something simple but having someone else take over that task may mean hours or days of figuring out what to do. Reduce the threat by documenting these tasks. Handing off the task with instructions makes the transition easier saving time and money.

Position Mismatches

Be careful when rewarding your staff with titles. Many small businesses give titles rather than raises when cash is short. The problem with giving titles to staff members that do not accurately describe the work they do is that now you have created a mismatch. You leave no room to bring in other more skilled people later when you need them. If your bookkeeper's title is CFO, what will you do when you need financial leadership beyond your bookkeeper's skills? Similarly, if the team member who provides people with access to your business applications is called your CIO and not your Systems Administrator, what will you do when you need a CIO to negotiate contracts, direct implementations and so on.

Giving your team members the right titles helps them move on when the time is right as well. People can get stuck when they have a title on their resume that does not reflect the work actually done. They may not be considered a fit for their next position. Consider the titles you have given your team so far and determine whether the titles and work requirements are a good fit. Check out the Position List in the back of the book if you need help.

Changing a Threat to an Asset

Things happen. People move on to other jobs or leave for a variety of reasons. Make sure that you can move on without your irreplaceable or single source of failure resources because you shifted the threat to an asset:

- Document what they do at a level that would make an equally skilled person successful.
- Train a replacement who can step up during vacations, holidays, and work overload.

- Present a plan for how the irreplaceable work can be done on vacations and holidays and then make sure your resource schedules one.
- Consider how you would replace each member of your team quickly so you have a plan in place.

Planning ahead and taking the steps to mitigate your risks make your business more resilient. Investors and bankers like to know that you are not vulnerable if key resources leave. You need to know that as well.

The Right Role for the Job

Accurate roles go hand-in-hand in helping you build stronger teams. Many small businesses start by hiring friends, acquaintances, and family and then figuring out what they can do. This is backward and often ends up with people in positions for which they are not fully qualified. Even in family businesses where the purpose of the business is to give family members work, it is important to first define the resources you need. Only then, place your family members in the position where they are a fit. By defining the role before you assign work, you create clear expectations.

Roles vary. Before defining a new role in your business, make these decisions:

- Employee or Contractor
- Full-time or Part-time
- Fractional Leaders or Executive Suite

Employee or Contractor

The benefit of employees is the consistent use of their time and skills. You have staff you can invest in and train building your resources into a reliable team. These resources often expect benefits. In exchange, they work under your supervision; you are in control of their hours and the tools and equipment they are allowed to use. Contractors come and go as agreed using their own equipment and setting their own hours. Often contractors relieve the load during projects that have defined start and end dates that require additional or especially skilled resources or during seasonal increases in business. They tend to supervise themselves and can be let go with no consequences. However, they may not be available at the exact moment you need them because they are free to take work from anyone.

Full-Time or Part-Time

The difference between full- and part-time resources seems obvious at first. Full-time employees have traditionally worked 40 or more hours a week. Part-time workers worked fewer hours in jobs that tended to require fewer skills. Many entrepreneurs now embrace part-time professionals as well. They may be graduate students, parents of young children, or recently retired professionals who are not quite ready to give up working altogether. They come with skills and experience but for personal reasons do not want to work full-time. These professionals meet the needs of small businesses who need professionals on a budget but often demand concessions about where, when, and how they are willing to work.

Fractional Leaders or Executive Suite

Fractional leaders resemble part-time C-suite and senior leadership professionals who provide strategic leadership services to businesses as a contractor not an employee. Look for fractional leaders with the wisdom and experience you need to fill skill and leadership gaps. Fractional leaders provide the right direction as a contracted partner not an employee. While your business may not have the budget or benefit package necessary to attract the right full-time executive today, you may find your budget does allow for just enough fractional guidance to move you forward toward your goals until you do.

Good fractional leaders have at least 15 years of experience with a track record of success. They have strong business networks that could benefit your small business. They tend to be experienced consultants or former executives who are in the middle or near the end of their careers. Some focus primarily on tackling specific problems. The best factional leaders are known as small business advocates and may also do work with programs that support small business. These leaders enjoy working with startups or growth stage companies.

How Does Fractional Leadership Work.   Businesses that use fractional leadership have part-time agreements that work in a variety of ways:

- One day per week for management team meetings
- One week per month for reporting and planning
- Retained hours per month to be used as needed
- One month a year to monitor the health of the company
- Temporary interim leadership during your extended vacations, long-term vacations
- Long-term coverage during hiring and selection of more permanent executives

Benefits of Fractional Leaders

Consider adding fractional leaders to your team to:

- Provide Credibility
- Avoid Leadership Gaps
- Create Change and Make Pivots
- Add Scalability
- Get a New Perspective

Provide Credibility

One of the most often expressed frustrations among business owners who are looking to grow quickly or win bigger contracts is lack of credibility. Before a client, investor, or banker takes a risk, they want to know the business has a reasonable chance of success. When you offer a business or growth plan that includes executives and key senior leaders in the right positions to guide larger business initiatives, you gain credibility.

Avoid Leadership Gaps

Small business owners can find sudden loss of leadership puts their organization in a precarious place pretty quickly. Finding the right person to serve as a full-time senior leader or executive can take weeks, even months. It is clear to see that one way to avoid leadership gaps is by using fractional leaders as interim leadership until you find just the right person for your permanent executive team.

Create Change and Make Pivots

Sudden emergencies such as pandemics or civil unrest can happen overnight. Changes in regulations or laws can sneak up quickly. The need to stay up with the times is a long-term priority. These are the times when you may find an expert who can help you look objectively at your business, your staff, and your opportunities the most helpful.

Add Scalability

Fractional leaders have already experienced the pitfalls of growth and change. They know how to clear obstacles and prepare in advance for complex challenges. It is clear to see how being able to turn to someone with experience can reduce risks as you grow.

Get a New Perspective

Adding any leaders to your team brings in new perspectives. It is easy to see that because fractional leaders are experienced at developing strategies for success and may have worked in multiple industries; these leaders are often prepared to help small business owners think outside of the box. These leaders often become mentors to business owners and/or members of their leadership team.

Organization Charting

Use an organizational chart like the one that follows (Figure 5.4) to outline your organization today and/or your planned organization tomorrow. Consider using two charts. One for now that identifies all positions needed or filled today and one that shows the positions required as the company grows according to your growth plan. Understanding the resources you need in advance keeps you from hiring people because you like them and not because you need them.

Your chart should look something like the example provided. The titles may be different, but the shape should be very similar. The hierarchy helps show who reports to whom so that there is no confusion among team members.

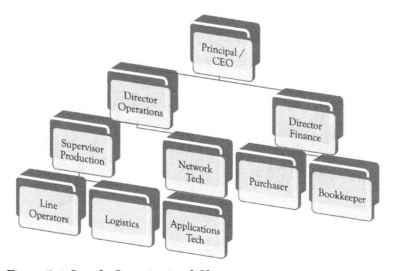

Figure 5.4 Sample Organizational Chart

Use real job titles in your chart. Some companies enjoy creating job titles that are fun and nontraditional. If your employees, clients, and customers are not going to need to find the right person to speak by asking for a title, there is little harm. Creative naming usually only works in very small organizations.

The benefit of predicting how your team may grow shows the ability to more accurately predict the cost of your operations. When you can predict the cost of your resources, those costs can then be included in your budget projections.

Uncovering Growth Options

Growing capacity means growing your business by expanding into new markets, building new opportunities, and/or improving the way you do business that better control your costs and is effective.

Here are some ways to expand your capacity you may not have considered:

- Government Contracting
- Accelerators and Incubators
- DEI Programs
- Mergers and Acquisitions

Government Contracting

The United States government invests in small and minority-owned businesses by setting aside a minimum of 3 to 5 percent of all federal contracting opportunities for small, women, minority, and veteran-owned businesses. Many years, the investment is higher. In 2018, the SBA announced, "The federal government exceeded its small business federal contracting goal for the sixth consecutive year, awarding 25.05 percent in federal contract dollars to small businesses totaling $120.8 billion, an increase from the previous fiscal year of nearly $15 billion." Most states have similar programs. (SBA 2019)

To qualify, businesses are required to undergo a certification process to prove eligibility and then register to bid. Certification and registration can be tedious and time consuming. The SBA provides resources to assist you in determining what certifications may be available to you. The SBA also provides free and low-cost training and guidance for small business owners going through the registration process.

Accelerator and Business Education Programs

Many corporations such as Capital One, Target, and Goldman Sachs set money aside for small business acceleration programs. There are multitudes of free and nearly free programs designed to educate and assist small businesses. Businesses who operate as part of their small business community often access accelerator and incubator programs to help fill in knowledge and skill gaps. Nonprofits that support business acceleration know that business owners are stronger together. These organizations believe that with the right connections and support offer you the opportunity to you grow your capacity.

It is never too soon or too late to invest in support and education. There are programs designed to fit every need. Investments in business education and training increase your credibility and make you more bankable while teaching you new skills that grow capacity. Find the right program for yourself in the list provided at CapacitySquared.net.

Diversity, Equity, and Inclusion

Many corporations reach out to small and diverse businesses with supplier diversity programs similar to government contracting programs in an effort to be more inclusive. These companies pledge a certain dollar amount of the company budget to the certified small veteran, women, and minority-owned businesses that might not otherwise be considered as vendors. Some corporations even pass the DEI requirement on to their larger vendors choosing vendors with their own supplier diversity programs more frequently.

According to the Harvard Business Review, "Some large companies encourage, and in some cases, require their suppliers to create their own diversity initiatives to broaden the impact. For instance, as of 2019, the retailer Target spent $1.4 billion on goods and services provided by first-tier diverse suppliers and influenced its first-tier suppliers to buy over $800,000 worth of offerings from second-tier diverse suppliers." (Bateman, Barrington, and Date 2020)

Getting access to DEI programs often requires some effort. Most corporations require program registration with a proof of certification similar to the government. Registration processes tend to be tedious and do not guarantee an opportunity. National registration programs attract mid-size organizations looking for small and diverse suppliers giving your company a broader chance at a match but may require paid memberships to be included.

Mergers and Acquisitions

Acquiring a competitor or merging with another small business provides another pathway to rapid growth you might consider. Acquisitions or mergers offer a variety of opportunities you might find attractive. Keep in mind, the transition of two companies into one must be handled carefully. The combination of two cultures, two sets of business processes, and two management styles into one new cohesive unit requires careful preparation.

For small companies, the planning and transition process cannot be taken for granted. When two small businesses come together, it can become quickly apparent that neither has the infrastructure to adequately operate the new larger entity. Change management considerations are even more important. Your larger business will likely need new management to drive new processes and procedures to move information efficiently, make decisions, and deliver on time.

Acquisition Reasons

There are many reasons for considering growth by acquisition or merger. Here are few:

- Market Share Expansion
- Scaling Up
- Discount Equipment Acquisition
- Supply Chain Flexibility
- DEI

Market Share Expansion

Whatever reason a business owner looks to make an acquisition, the added benefit can be a new list of customers. A loyal customer base is a valuable asset. Of course, making sure the customer base is loyal is the key. The purchase of a troubled company can come with customers who are not willing to trust the new owner and make the transition. Additionally, the purchase of a company that already sold several times may leave customers change weary and disloyal. Success requires careful upfront investigation and proper transition planning to encourage and support customers in making the transition.

Scale Up

Scaling up, to meet growing demands, can be tricky especially in a tight labor market. Finding labor with the necessary skills, onboarding, and training can be time consuming and expensive. You might consider rapidly adding resources in locations where those resources are most needed by merging or acquiring a local business.

In the right circumstances, growing your resources through merger or acquisition can be the answer to meeting a host of opportunities. Consulting and service companies often add to their ranks by buying or merging with competitors or strategic partners with a strong customer base. Not only do they get a new set of potential customers, but they also get skilled resources the customers already trust.

Discount Equipment Acquisition

Adding necessary equipment can be one of the more expensive aspects of rapid growth for your business. For struggling businesses, the equipment may be the most valuable asset on the books. Getting access to the equipment you need through a merger or acquisition often comes with skilled resources who know the equipment. Additionally, you may get the added bonus of new customers as well.

Keep in mind that the used equipment comes with some risk. Find out if a merger or acquisition impacts warranties. If the equipment is new enough to have a warranty, the transition of ownership sometimes voids those agreements. Make sure your attorney reviews all contracts so that you know where you stand.

Supply Chain Flexibility

Sometimes, the answer to your supply chain problems is to own more of the chain. If you cannot get the materials, you need to produce your product because the resources are limited then owning the resources is one way to solve the problem.

For example, a fracking company sporadically needed a lot of sand. Because of the nature of the business, the need for sand was hard to predict. The sand was not easy to store. It needed to be purchased without notice. When they needed sand, they needed it in huge quantities and the need was urgent. They were often delayed waiting for suppliers who gave priority to buyers that were more consistent.

The company solved the problem by purchasing a sandlot. It seemed easy enough; when the fracking company needed the sand, they could get it. When they did not need the sand, they had plenty of buyers for the remainder, which they sold at a discount. The fracking company had never intended to be in the sand business. However, it was the most expedient way to meet a pressing need.

Due Diligence

Before agreeing to merge or acquire another business carefully investigate your target. Understanding why the business is for sale may tell you a bit about the value. You want to know as much as you can about why the owner is choosing to sell and what the true value of the company is today.

A detailed operational assessment audit may reveal information you might miss during negotiations. It pays to understand not just the company financials, but also details about how the other functions important to success are carried out as well. The information you need may be different depending on the business and industry you are targeting. Free checklists are available on the Internet. Take the responsibility to do your research making sure you are getting the value you deserve out of your investment.

Information you should know includes but may not be limited to:

- Obligations including (equity, contracts, licenses, rents, and so on)
- Legal actions (current and likely)
- Technology (contracts, licenses, and bandwidth requirements)
- Inventory and material management (if applicable)
- Organization chart
- Business strategy
- Employee benefits and management

- Marketing and sales strategy
- Reputation
- Financials
- Assets

Pro Forma

As you consider an expansion, it is important to understand the difference between pro forma financial reports and those created following generally accepted accounting principles sometimes referred to as Generally Accepted Accounting Principles (GAAP). Pro forma reports often leave out one-time expenses such as formation fees, restructuring costs, and cash real estate purchases. Pro forma reports sometimes help determine a more accurate view of the future by excluding costs that are not likely to recur. However, it pays to view or create pro forma reports with great care including notes about what has been removed so that reviewers agree that the reports are reliable.

CHAPTER 6

Cycles

If you really look closely most overnight successes took a long time.

—Steve Jobs

Utilizing Business Life Cycles

Successful entrepreneurs know how to focus. Business leaders of growing businesses need focus in a world that provides plenty of distractions. Everything you do in your business moves your opportunity closer or further away from your end goal. The decisions you make about your opportunity impact every business decision you make.

Understanding Cycles

Organized cycles are best suited to exploring and implementing an opportunity supported by a growth plan or a project. A well-designed systemic approach integrates people, data, business systems, and processes so that each phase well timed and handled smoothly. An organized approach helps maintain focus. Your business is most likely to succeed when every opportunity fits into your vision and can be accomplished as a part of your mission as you step toward your end goal.

Additionally, cycles make change easier. It seems counter intuitive. However, the greatest inhibitor of innovation is risk. Cycles create a structure that reduces the risk of innovation by stopping bad ideas before money and time are wasted while perfecting promising ideas before costly rework is necessary.

Make your cycle(s) fit in your business strategy and not the other way around. The most elegant cycle does not take the place of a good business strategy. You may however find gaps in your strategy more obvious and easier to address as you work through cycles that rely on best practices for success.

These include:

- Product Development Life Cycle (PLC) (Figure 6.1)
- Project Development Life Cycle (PDLC)
- System Development Life Cycle (SDLC)
- Opportunity Development Life Cycle (ODLC)

PLC

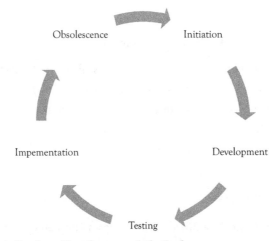

Figure 6.1 Product Development Life Cycle

A PLC is sometimes referred to as Product Life Cycle Management to avoid being confused with a project cycle. The product cycle begins with the idea and ends with product retirement often call obsolesces. These cycles may be customized and often have five to seven phases. Manufacturing and implementation are often the longest phases and include business systems and processes, and data management as well.

Benefits include:

- Shortening launch times
- Gathering requirements to help ensure functionality matches needs
- Predicting costs
- Managing budgets and timelines more accurately

- Reducing risks
- Making key adjustments possible
- Improving chances of success
- Quantifying expected results
- Requiring proper testing before release
- Providing information necessary for more accurate planning
- Utilizing more thought in change management

PDLC

Figure 6.2 Project Development Life Cycle

Projects are dedicated efforts designed to meet a specific goal with a pre-dicted start and end date. Projects can be simple or very complex and elaborate. They may be short or take years to complete. The (PDLC) (Figure 6.2) follows a systemic approach that helps ensure success. One or more projects governed by a PDLC can be included in a PLC or an ODLC.

Projects are organized into four phases including initiation, planning, execution, and closure. Initiation encompasses defining goals, estimating costs, and determining the scope. The planning phase sets deadlines and priorities, considers risks, creates a timeline based on defined tasks, and identifies the resources required. The execution phase includes assigning resources to tasks, monitoring work, managing changes and risks, and reporting performance. Finally, the last stage, closure affirms that goals were reached in alignment with the agreed upon scope and captures lessons learned.

Benefits include:

- Avoiding scope creep
- Offering more detailed plans and timelines
- Quantifying expected results
- Ensuring appropriate documentation
- Predicting costs

- Managing risks
- Making key adjustments possible to improve chances of success
- Utilizing amore thought in change management

Sometimes, people confuse the System Development Life Cycle (SDLC) (Figure 6.3) with the PDLC. Like other development cycles, the SDLC provides a systemic methodical process. However, the SDLC focuses very specifically on developing software as quickly as possible in an iterative way. An SDLC is sometimes part of a PDLC.

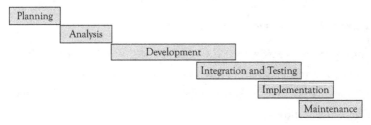

Figure 6.3 Software Development Life Cycle

Software development is typically organized in seven phases that include planning, analysis, design, development, integration and testing, implementation, and maintenance that may overlap. The SDLC begins with planning which identifies resources, estimates costs, builds a timeline, and identifies tasks necessary for success. The design phase identifies requirements, determines specifications, and documents features and functionality. The development phase is essentially the same as an execution phase in other cycles including assigning resources to tasks, monitoring work, managing changes and risks, and reporting performance. The integration and testing phase is unique in that software must be carefully tested before integrating it into a production environment to avoid unforeseen consequences. Integration allows users access to the software. The maintenance phase allows for iterative improvements that include fixing issues that have come up after implementation and making updates to improve the quality of the software.

Benefits include:

- Providing iterative opportunities for improvement
- Gathering requirements to help ensure functionality matches needs
- Making key adjustments to improve chances of success along the way
- Quantifying expected results
- Requiring proper testing before release
- Providing documentation essential for success
- Utilizing best practices in change management
- Reducing risks and costs

ODLC

The ODLC provides a systemic cycle supporting the growth of capacity by taking advantage of new business opportunities. The ODLC often improves the timing of each step from initiation to review in five phases. These phases include initiation, planning, execution, implementation, and review.

The ODLC moves from beginning to end in an orderly fashion reducing risks and costs. Like other cycles, this best practice model supports better decision making. Taking time up front to consider the full ramifications of development and implementation often reduces time to market and cut costs by giving your team time to work through any issues up front. Because opportunities involve developing or creating new products or services, the ODLC may include one or more of the other cycles as well.

Benefits include:

- Abandoning bad opportunities early
- Managing budgets more accurately
- Including funding as a necessary element of success
- Making key adjustments to improve chances of success
- Ensuring better decision making
- Quantifying expected results

- Providing information necessary for more accurate planning
- Offering more detailed planning and design
- Clarifying strategies
- Utilizing better development and implementation strategies
- Helping to control costs and reduce risks

Cycle Phases

Cycle phases may last just days or go on for months depending on complexity. For the cycles to be of full benefit, you must go through all the phases. Repeat cycle phases if necessary, being sure that you are ready to move on before you go ahead. Customize the order slightly making sure the cycle meets your needs. For example, planning always comes before funding in an ODLC. Without a business or growth plan, no one should give you money and it is not wise to invest your own. That said planning and funding sometimes come before design when appropriate.

Go/No Go Decisions

A go/no go decision is just what it sounds like. It is a point where you and your leadership team consider whether the investment is worth the cost and risks associated. If an opportunity is not going to turn out as hoped, you want to abandon or modify it as quickly as possible so that you can focus your resources on products and/or services will. Stopping on paper is much less expensive than failing during development. Stopping during development is again less expensive than failing after implementation.

If you have to go back to the drawing board, you want to do it as quickly as possible. One iteration of an idea can lead to another making what you end up with more successful than it might otherwise have been. There are a lot of good business ideas not all of them should be done. Use Go/No Go moments to avoid disasters.

For example, a trucking company was about to make a large purchase of new vehicles to meet the needs of a new client when it found out that vehicle regulations were about to change. The company owner decided to lease vehicles to meet their client's need at the start to test the new relationship and see how regulations might impact their purchase.

The client relationship worked out. Six months down the road, the regulations did change. When they were confident in making a purchase, the new vehicles met the new standards. If they had purchased the vehicles earlier, they would have been forced to make expensive modifications.

Using an ODLC

As important as all of the life cycles are, small businesses most often rely on opportunities when expanding capacity. Many entrepreneurs move forward without using a systemic approach, thus decreasing their chances of success. For this reason alone, walking through this particular cycle, phase by phase, makes sense (Figure 6.4).

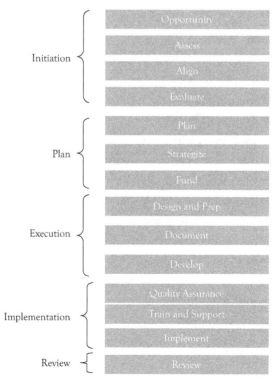

Figure 6.4 Opportunity Development Life Cycle

Phase One—Initiation

Figure 6.5 Opportunity Development Life Cycle phase one

Every idea should be vetted—EVERY idea, whether you are considering starting a new business or adding a product or service to your existing business. It is NEVER too late to assess, align, and evaluate the viability of your opportunity(ies).

Opportunity

An opportunity statement (Figure 6.6) explains a need that is not met and how that need impacts your potential customer as discussed earlier. It also clarifies how your solution best meets that need. When you put a statement in writing, you gain clarity. Here are some examples:

- Members of my small community complain they cannot get good coffee nearby and they have no place to gather which makes them feel isolated. This is why I am opening a gourmet coffee shop with comfortable group seating that encourages coming together throughout the day to experience community.
- Many companies recognize they need a way to communicate instantly even while remote that provides more privacy than a public chat. We are developing a chat room with an instant side conversation feature that has video options. This feature allows you to ping one or more members of your group for a quick private chat with no additional meeting invitations or setup required.
- Climate change impacts us all by causing more frequent storms with devastating floods in some areas and extreme

droughts in others. Therefore, we propose building a channel system that pipes rising waters from flood prone areas to
drought stressed lakes and reservoirs hundreds of miles away.
Our solution reduces the risk of flooding while helping to
meet the water needs of drought-stricken communities.

Focus on what your opportunity promises to deliver and follow the
steps to write your own opportunity statement.

Step One—Write Your Statement

Write one to three sentences that describe what the need is and how you
can resolve the need. Keep the sentences so simple a seventh grader could
understand. Do not worry about making your statement perfect yet. You
may want to revise your statement later. Use the template for guidance
(Figure 6.6).

> *[The Customer]* has this [problem] that causes *[this pain/inconvenience]*.
> This is why *[my solution]* meets the need *[how]*.

Figure 6.6 Opportunity Statement template

Step Two—Evaluate Your Statement

Now evaluate your statement. Is your statement in alignment with your
mission, your vision, and your values? If not, consider what changes need
to be made and rewrite your statement.

Assess

Taking time to break down and assess the opportunity on which your
business relies or will rely offers many insights that help drive your business strategy. What you learn may cause you to pivot or shift in ways you
might never have considered. A sound opportunity evaluation of your
ongoing business provides confirmation that your opportunity is a good
match for your business.

Considering the Match

Carefully assessing your opportunity makes sense to be sure you are on the right path. Small business owners tend to have limited resources and therefore taking a moment to answer these questions for yourself or as a leadership team can save time, resources, and money.

Based on what you know, now consider these questions:

- Is the opportunity still worth pursuing?
- Is your idea a good match with your mission, vision, and values?
- Will it move you forward to your end goal?
- Does it fit in the market you identified?
- Can you see a path to success?

Go/No Go Decision

Based on your answers, consider now if the opportunity is a good match.

Yes. Yes is the easy answer. Once you know your business is a good match then you are ready to move forward and begin.

No. If it does not then ask yourself if you need to expand your vision and mission or if this opportunity is not a match after all. If not then it is a No Go. Move on quickly to something else.

Maybe. If the opportunity is not a perfect match but you have already invested time and money, you should not just quit. Instead consider whether you can make your opportunity a better fit. Can you expand your mission or vision? Can you modify the opportunity to be a better match?

Align

Once you determine the idea is worth further investigation, it is time to ask the harder questions. It is clear to see that moving forward with a new opportunity has some risk. Because there is risk involved, it makes sense to spend some time carefully considering what all is involved. You want to know the opportunity is a good fit for your business. You must validate that the product or service is legal and can meet local state, and federal regulations.

Contemplating the Fit

The next step is to consider if the opportunity fits in with the talents/ skills, resources, and interests of your business. Take a moment to answers these questions for yourself or as a leadership team.

- Do we have team members with the talents/skills to make this opportunity successful?
- Can our current team meet the increased demand of this opportunity?
- Who might we need to add to our team to be successful?
- What equipment/software is necessary to support the opportunity?
- What equipment/software must be purchased or accounts added?
- Can we compete with the projected added costs of new team members, equipment, and/or software?
- Is this opportunity in alignment with our interests congruent with our values and goals?

Determining Legality

Consider whether your product/service can be sold where and how you want to offer it to your potential customers. Americans tend to view the United States as one big whole. When it comes to commerce, it is really more than 50 different parts. State regulations and laws may vary greatly. Sometimes state laws and regulations are not consistent with federal laws and regulations. Federal laws always trump state laws. However, if you are in a heavily regulated industry where the courts are in the process of making a decision, just know decisions can go back and forth. You may be in limbo while you wait to see who wins. If you have doubts, seek competent legal advice from an attorney with experience in your field.

Go/No Go Decision

Yes. Once you confirm you have no hurdles in your way you are ready to move forward.

No. If your opportunity has legal hurdles you cannot overcome then now is the time to move on to something better suited for your company.

Maybe. Perhaps there are barriers in your way that can be moved. You cannot afford to ignore them. If you have the time and budget to clear those hurdles, the opportunity may still be a go.

For example, Fred Smith had an idea about creating a point to point shipping company first documented in a college paper. He got a C. The idea was not a good fit for the industry in 1970 because there were regulatory and legal hurdles. Still Smith went forward with an opportunity that many thought would never succeed. The company took off in 1977 during airline deregulation. The journey from startup to success was expensive and time consuming, but today his company is a household name, Federal Express. (Murray 2019)

Determine if you can make changes or remove barriers that would make your opportunity a go. If not, move on quickly to something else.

Evaluate

Your opportunity must be able to capture enough market share to make moving forward a good idea. Even if you considered your market when picking your opportunity, a more thorough market evaluation is essential in confirming you have a viable opportunity now. The information you gather during your evaluation helps create a more successful market strategy.

The evaluation helps you better understand your buyer or target. Once you know your buyer, you are poised to evaluate your competitors to understand how they reach your target. Understanding your competitor's strategies often helps you understand how you can reach your target customers more effectively.

Now it is time to take a closer look and evaluate your:

- Market
- Buyer
- Competitors

Market Evaluation. For every market, there is a set of customers. You need a big enough share of those customers to be successful. Determine the size of the share you need by looking at where your product or service belongs in your target market. If the market is large, you may need just a small percentage of buyers. If you have a smaller total market, you may need to capture a larger portion.

For example, if you are one of two plumbers in a small community then you may want to capture 50 percent or more of the market. If you provide software as a service (SaaS) with a target market of 10 million, you may only need 5 percent as your share. Often, entrepreneurs capture a small share of a large market providing goods and services as a part of a niche opportunity. Your evaluation may lead you to a market of more specialized customer needs too small for larger corporations to spend time and money building but just big enough for you to target.

Success is driven by knowing how big your market is and how to get your share. This is why understanding what makes your opportunity unique is so important. There are four categories of potential customers in any given market:

- Can and willing to pay
- Interested but only at a certain price point
- Willing but unable to pay
- Willing but blocked by government laws and regulations

It is tempting to consider EVERYONE willing or interested as a part of your target market but doing so may cause you to make decisions based on false assumptions. Only customers willing and able to pay are your target market. Exclude potential customers who want your product and/or service but cannot or will not pay a fair price. Additionally, exclude customers who cannot buy your product and/or service because it violates local, state, or government regulations or laws. These customers are blocked.

Define Your Market Category. Goods or services are most often sold in three distinct groups often referred to by their three-letter acronyms:

- Business-to-Consumer (B2C)—Your business sells to some portion of the general public often referred to as consumers
- Business-to-Business (B2B)—Your business sells to other businesses
- Business-to-Government (B2G)—Your business sells to the government which includes municipalities, local, state, and federal entities

Determine which category best fits your business to better understand your target.

Determine Market Saturation. Research the industry to determine how big the market is today. Use readily available data such as data provided by trade journals, U.S. Bureau of Labor and Statistics, U.S. Chamber of Commerce, and the U.S. Census Bureau to determine your industry outlook. Gauge whether the market has room for one more competitor sometimes referred to as market saturation.

Buyer Evaluation. Within each category, there are one or more buyers. Buyers' need(s) tend to be similar. By identifying your buyer's need(s), you start to identify your best target. The better you identify your buyer, the more likely you are to make a sell.

Understanding your buyer creates value. Investors are more likely to invest in companies that accurately define their market and describe their buyers. Loan officers prefer lending to entrepreneurs that are clear as well.

Not only that, but large buyers trust companies who understand their market which in turn leads to larger contracts.

While there are a few businesses which just start and serve a need so perfectly they fall into a niche and never have to think about marketing, those are few and far between. Even if you do not need investors, a loan, or you do not need or want large contracts, it is clear to see that understanding your target buyers is valuable because better understanding brings greater success.

Objectively identifying your buyer and determining the value and consistency of the need helps you make better business decisions. Often, entrepreneurs think they have their target buyers figured out only to be surprised after a closer evaluation. The information gathered during your evaluation helps to create a more successful market strategy that more accurately targets the buyers who care about your product or service.

Learn everything possible about your buyer. It may seem that your buyer is obvious or that your service is so simple that understanding your buyer is not important. This is never true. Once you understand the obvious need, it pays to dig deeper to figure out what it is your buyer wants.

Making a profile of each potential buyer helps you define your market. Who wants what you have to offer and why? Answer these questions about each potential buyer:

- **Point of Pain/Inconvenience**
  What is the biggest challenge/pain point your buyer faces that your product or service resolves?
- **Match**
  What makes the customer a good match for your product or service at the proposed price?
- **Who**
  What are your potential buyer demographics?

Point of Pain/Inconvenience. There is some point of pain, absence of joy, or wish for convenience being experienced by your potential customer. The experience is enough for your target customer to consider spending money. Understanding what within reason means to your potential customer sometimes makes the difference between success and failure.

Match. A buyer is a match when the buyer has both the will AND the ability to make a purchase. Matches are essential to success. Make the extra effort to be clear. Better understanding what makes a match can be the key to success. Buyers in different demographic segments tend to make buying decisions in similar ways. It is clear to see how understanding that can be helpful when you develop your marketing strategy.

Buyers are always ultimately people. Even if your buyer is technically a business or a government entity, a real person or group of people makes the decision to buy or contract your goods and/or services. Even when your end buyer is a consumer, you may need a distributor to get your products on a shelf. Understanding the typical people who work in the buyer/contractor role helps make you more successful at providing a product they do not just need but they also want.

Think about a restaurant. The product is a delicious meal. The buyer is a hungry customer. It might seem on the surface that this is as much as a business owner needs to know. Yet, there is so much more to understand. If the restaurant caters corporate events, the path toward a attracting a customer is quite different from the path toward attracting a family of four. If the restaurant is expensive, the experience of luxury service may be the inspiration to purchase. The path to attracting those luxury dining customers is different than attracting a family of four to a casual dining restaurant.

Large restaurant chains know this. They invest hundreds of thousands of dollars in understanding their buyer. Chains know that when they invest in the opportunity to open a new restaurant, they must select the right location. Restaurant do better close to the clientele most likely to come. Restaurant chains know that where is as important as what if they are to attract their buyer. To answer the question of where, they carefully profile their customers so they can first understand who. This kind of research often yields surprises.

Consider Brinker International which started out with Chili's, a nationally known upscale hamburger restaurant. What they learned when studying their most likely buyers was interesting. They understood their buyer was typically a middle-class or upper middle-class family with two income earners. These patrons would pay more for a hamburger served in an interesting environment. They also knew that these busy families were unlikely to drive very far for a week day meal. Competitors that were more than 10 miles away were not very competitive.

Researchers discovered these buyers liked variety. No matter how good the food, interesting the restaurant, and great the service, their buyers did not go to the same venue every time. They noticed new Chili's outlets soon brought competitors who often took a portion of the market because Chili's customers like variety.

The answer to this problem soon became clear. Brinker needed to provide the variety buyers wanted. Armed with this information, Brinker created a strategy of building a variety of Brinker restaurants near the same location. When their buyers went out, they would be far more likely to choose a Brinker restaurant. They asked their buyer what are you hungry for? Once they understood, they provided their buyer with what they wanted most, variety.

It does not matter if you sell SaaS, you are a plumber, a lawyer, or a brick layer. When you understand your buyer, you become better able to determine more exactly not just what the need is, but what your buyer wants. Understanding the need while fulfilling the want helps you develop a competitive edge.

Sometimes there is a very small and specific market. Your buyer can be easily profiled. Other times you may need to create several profiles to understand who each of your potential buyers are now.

Needs tend to be easier to understand than wants. A want has more to do with values. Wants motivate behavior. All people want their basic needs served such as connection, physical well-being, honesty, safety, pleasure/play, peace, and meaning according to Marshall Rosenburg PhD (Rosenberg 2003).

In a 2021 Korn Ferry, a global organizational consulting firm conducted a study in which buyers reported that two of the top three behaviors most important during the sales process were to understand the buyer's business situation, respond to needs, and actively listening. Buyers want to be understood. They want to feel heard. Korn Ferry suggested that the most important question to ask is, "Are you actively showing up where your buyers are buying?" (Korn Ferry 2021) To know, you have to know who those buyers are and what they want and need. Consider who may need and want your product and begin to build a buyer profile by researching buyers who buy similar products.

In the marketplace, knowledge is power. Buyer profiles help provide that knowledge. Picture your customers as if you are describing each of them to someone else. Build a profile for each type to better understand who they are and why they would buy from your business. Once you understand your customer, you are ready to design marketing channels that will become the basis for your marketing strategy.

Learn the following things about your likely buyers to build a profile:

- Age
- Education
- Gender
- Income
- Habits
- Values
- Priorities
- Wants
- Location

Age

No product or service meets the needs AND wants of every age group. Children have different needs than adults. Working adults have different needs than retired adults. There are generational differences in how purchasing decisions are likely to be made as well. When you understand that and use a market strategy on target with the age range of potential decision-making buyers, you often have an edge over those who do not.

Education

The importance of education varies based on the product and/or service. Still you may find that the wants of more educated consumers are different than those with less education even for the same product. For example, everyone at some time needs a plumber whether they have a PhD or they failed to graduate from high school. One may care more about pricing and the other may care more about security. Targeting marketing to each profile is more likely to be successful than a generic advertising piece sent to each potential buyer.

Gender

When a product and/or service attraction is gender specific, the difference is generally clear to see. When you market to both men and women, the needs and wants may vary. It pays to make sure you target the individual needs and wants of each gender in your strategy. Increase your market share by speaking to those differences.

Income

Understanding how much money the buyer/company has to budget and how much of that budget is available to purchase your product and/or service informs your market strategy right down to the best words to use to get a buyer's attention. Luxury brands may focus on aesthetics while economy brands focus on durability and savings. As economic times change, so do successful marketing strategies. If you pay attention, you soon notice that in lean economic times marketing strategies shift toward value even for luxury items. This is true for B2C, B2G, and B2B products and services. Buyers of all kinds are impacted by their environment. When budgets are tight at home, B2B and B2G budgets tend to become tight as well.

Habits

Understanding the buying habits or repeatable patterns that surround the decision to purchase your product or service provides an edge. Some of those habits include company and government protocols. Even if your market is B2B or B2G, buyers have buying habits. Be aware that buyers who purchase on behalf of a company or a government agency have needs to fulfill that may be more career oriented.

Values

Understanding what your potential customer values helps you make decisions not just about how to market your product or service but how to produce it as well. Any buyer concerned about climate change may be drawn to more sustainable products and/or services. Ads that use words that reiterate your customers' value-based needs tend to be most effective. Images and symbols that reflect those values may be important as well. For example, many products use patriotic symbols and images in packaging and promotions to attract attention. Remember buyers are, after all, people who buy things no matter whom they buy them for on any given day.

Priorities

Buyers tend to care more about discounts in harsh economic times even when they are spending the company's money and not their own. All buyers are affected by the economic climate, competing priorities, and media too. Buyer priorities change. Buyers cannot help but be impacted by their overall environment. For example, during the Covid-19 pandemic, safety considerations became huge concerns even where safety had not been a priority before.

Wants

Do not confuse wants with needs. Needs make your buyer consider purchasing your product or service. Someone may need a handbag. Wants often are the deciding factor in determining which one to purchase. One buyer may want a designer name, another sparkles, and yet another a well-made bag at a good price.

The same is true of services. A company may need a consultant to handle a merger. One company may want local resources who understand the business community and culture. Another may want consultants who are experts in mergers and understand the marketplace and complexities of integrations. The want guides the final decision.

Location

Marketing to a global marketplace is very different than marketing to local customers. It is easy to see that it is important to know where your customer is and how to reach them. If you are offering trade services, you may wish to provide your services in only a 100 mile radius. Your marketing strategy must be very specific to your area. If you provide a product that can be shipped nationwide, you are going to have to catch the attention of buyers in a very different way. If you provide services remotely, then it is possible you could focus anywhere in the world. You may care more about time zones and Internet connections than where you physically do business.

Using the Demographics. Once you identify your buyers, it makes sense that you are more likely to build a market strategy that appeals more directly to them. When you understand not just their needs, but their wants, you connect with them better. Because you made the effort to get to know your target market, you can build a market strategy that is more effective.

Competitor Evaluation

Few markets are so small that entrepreneurs have no competition except for local products and services in very rural areas. Even so, no matter where you are or how broad your market small business, owners and leaders like you find understanding what your competitors have to offer helpful. A better understanding helps you prioritize your product or service features and helps you properly price.

Even if you have been in business for a long time, it pays to look at where your business fits in comparison with your competition. Understanding your competitors helps you ascertain their unique business advantages. This helps you ensure what you have to offer meets the needs and wants of your target market better than your competitors. Your business becomes more resilient because you know where you fit.

Consider doing a competitive analysis at least once a year so that you begin identifying trends over time. Some trends may indicate that changes are happening quickly and others may show buying shifts that happen slowly over multiple years. If you are paying attention, your team will be more likely to respond to changing trends. You may even come up with the next innovation that shakes the market.

Benefits. There are additional benefits to understanding who your competitors are such as:

- Determine Industry Interest to Investors
- Learn from Startup Data
- Define Your Competitive Edge
- Identify New Opportunities
- Understand Market Changes
- Learn from Competitor Mistakes
- Understand Competitor Metrics
- Determine Digital Footprint
- Check Pricing Assumptions
- Identify Possible Gaps
- Prioritize Development
- Acquire Disrupters

Interest Investors. Even if you are not looking for outside investment and you are not planning to get a loan, taking a look at your competition through the eyes of investors provides valuable information. Understanding what characteristics your competitors have that make them worthy of investment helps you set your own priorities. Better understanding who investors think has a future also helps you define what makes your opportunity different, even better than your competition.

It is easy to see that if you are seeking investment, this research is even more powerful. When you see the types of investors who have already shown interest in your competitors, you better understand who might be interested in you. Investors know that if you understand your competitors, you are primed to compete.

Learn From Startup Data. Get valuable information from previous startups. A little research may show you what your initial investment should be at the beginning. You may get a better idea of how much capital you require. You may uncover where your best sources for raising capital are likely to be as well. Your competitors may even be willing to tell you how they became successful and give you good advice on how to be successful yourself, if they do not see you as a threat.

Define Your Competitive Edge. When you compare mission statements, products, services, integrations, and anything else that make your competitors stand out, you start to identify what makes you different and better. Make note of those differences.

Identify New Opportunities. Seeing that others have recognized the same needs that you recognized in your opportunity validates your assumption that a market exists. Understanding how your competitors meet those needs sometimes identifies areas of interest you might have missed.

Understand Market Changes. By using your first competitive analysis as a benchmark and then doing semiannual or annual reviews, you start to be able to predict market changes. Watching your competitors over time, you may soon find you and your team are less likely to be surprised and more likely to benefit from marketplace changes.

If you find yourself in a rapidly changing market, take a look at how your competitors are pivoting to give you more direction about how to successfully pivot yourself. You create an advantage when you look for opportunities to better serve your customers' changing needs.

Learn From Competitor Mistakes. Mistakes are costly. Identifying competitor errors helps you avoid the same pitfalls. When you learn from your competitor's mistakes, you save valuable time and money.

Understand Competitor Metrics. Metrics such as revenue and market share help identify where your competitor fits in your market. If someone has your share of the market now, it does not mean you are at an end. After all most of the teens in the United States were on My Space before they went to Facebook and then shifted to Twitter, tweeting their every movement prior to moving again to TikTok and Instagram. Things change.

Understanding how long it took for a competitor to grow and reach revenue and market goals helps you plan. Looking at competitor budgets and sales predictions provides data that assists you in making more reliable predictions yourself. Clearly understanding your competitors gives you an advantage over others entering your marketplace who do not.

Determine Your Digital Footprint. Additionally, competitor research may tell you how big your digital footprint should be based on the size and type of your business. All companies must have a website. EVEN if you do not sell online and your customers do not go there much, it is likely they will when considering buying from you the first time. Additionally, websites have become one of the first sources of legitimacy potential investors and bankers look at to be sure you are for real. Vendors may check your website as well before making large orders.

Knowing where your competitors are on social media is important too. Understanding how useful online marketing is in your business segment can be extremely helpful. Knowing where your customers buy determines whether or not you must consider ecommerce options. Many small businesses have found success by making remote ordering and purchasing available months or even years before larger competitors.

Check Pricing Assumptions. Understanding how your competitors price is important. Research your competitors to understand what customers really pay. If there are bulk purchase discounts or loyalty pricing, you want to know. Validating your pricing strategy helps ensure your company stays viable in the marketplace.

Identify Possible Gaps. Use competitors' gaps to make your product and/or service better. Customer complaints often reveal missing features, functions, or services customers may be looking for now. These complaints uncover what is missing in the quest to satisfy potential customers. Understanding where others fail provides the opportunity to tweak your opportunity to fulfill unmet needs.

Prioritize Development. Once you have your best understanding of your customers' unmet needs, you are better prepared to prioritize development according to what your customers care about most. You are better set to make good planning decisions when you have to make a choice between implementing all at once or a little at a time.

Acquire Disrupters. When you recognize an innovation that is likely to disrupt the marketplace, you benefit in a couple of ways. If you are the disrupter suddenly being noticed by your bigger competitors, you have the chance to be acquired at a very nice profit. If you are the larger competitor noticing a disruption starting, you may be the one to acquire the innovation by purchasing your competitor.

Evaluating Competitors. Complete the steps that follow to evaluate your competitors.

Step One—Select Competitors

Start with five competitors. Evaluate a variety of your competition and not just the competitors that mirror your organization. Consider competitors that are similar to you first of course. Then look for those that are smaller and larger. Consider those competitors who are both direct and indirect. Direct competitors meet the same need(s) in the same ways. Indirect competitors meet the same need(s) in a different way. You may know your industry well and finding five competitors may be no trouble at all. If not, a quick browser search should provide all you need.

Step Two—Answer the Questions Below

Here are ten questions you should ask yourself about your competitors (Table 6.1):

1. Who are they? List three to five.
2. Which are most similar to your business?
3. How big is their share of the market?
4. Are your competitors growing? If so, how fast?
5. What is the biggest need your competitors meet for their customers?
6. What complaints of your competitor are most common?
7. What make you unique from your competitor?
8. What is your competitive edge or the one or two things you do better?
9. Why would someone choose your competitor over you?
10. What can you learn from your competitor's financials?
11. Who are/were their investors?

Step Three—Create a Spreadsheet

Table 6.1 Competitor Evaluation

Company Name	Category*	Number Customers	Investors	Revenue	Pricing	Differentiators	Complaints	Market Share

*(big, small, direct, indirect, different industry)

Note—If your opportunity includes more than one product or service, you may want to review each separately.

Step Four—Complete the Spreadsheet

Gather all the information you can find on each of your five or more competitors in your Competitor Evaluation spreadsheet (Table 6.1). Most of the time, this level of investigation can be done quickly. Publicly held companies publish the information in their annual reports. Private companies may provide answers on LinkedIn, online sites that publish hiring information, or even their own company websites. If you need additional help there are online tools available that are free, offer free trials, or are low cost. Find a list of those tools kept up-to-date on CapacitySquared.net (Table 6.2).

Table 6.2 Competitor Evaluation extended

Co Name	Cat*	# Cust	Rev	Pricing	Differentiators	Complaints	Market Share	Competitive Advantages	Insights

*(big, small, direct, indirect, different industry)

Step Five—Review Your Answers

Add two new columns now entitled Our/My Competitive Advantage and Insights. It may help to highlight these two new columns with a different background to easily tell your competitor's product or service from your opportunity.

Go/No Go Decision

Now that you know what, to whom, and at what price you have hit another Go/No Go moment, consider these questions:

- Would customers pay to meet the need that inspires your opportunity?
- Can your product or service be delivered at a competitive price?
- Can you make a profit in your market?

Yes. If yes, then you are ready to move ahead and consider what strategies work best for your market.

No. If no, then it is time to move on to a new opportunity.

Maybe. Work back through your opportunity starting with what and determine if changes or revisions to your opportunity make it viable.

Phase Two—Plan

Figure 6.7 Opportunity Development Life Cycle phase two

Plan

Plan a path to success. Once you know that your opportunity is viable build a five year plan to guide you to success (Figure 6.7). Operating any business is an intense process. A good plan is an excellent investment. A study entitled, *The Multiple Effects of Business Planning on New Venture Performance* reported in the *Journal of Management Studies* found that "companies that plan grow 30 percent faster than those that don't plan." This study found that though businesses found success without planning, businesses with a plan grew faster and were more successful than those that did not. (Burke, Fraser, and Greene 2010)

For this reason, it is clear to see a plan benefits you. The two most common plans are a business plan and a growth plan. Most entrepreneurs and business leaders have heard of a business plan. Not as many have heard of a growth plan. Both are useful in the right circumstances. Find an outline for each type of plan in the Appendix or start with a template for each at CapacitySquared.net.

Business Plan

A business plan remains the most commonly used plan for startups. Use a business plan as a blueprint to move forward for 3, 5, or 10 years. Five years is the most common timeframe. Ten years is a long time in today's rapidly changing world. Three years may not provide enough time in your timeline to meet goals.

These plans set specific business and revenue goals. Business plans include high-level strategies, analysis of opportunities, and identification of risks. A business plan also includes a timeline for goals that becomes the beginning of a roadmap for success. Most importantly, revenue projections offer the opportunity to track financial progress.

Growth Plan

A business plan and a growth plan cover many of the same things. A growth plan also includes details about the implementation of your opportunity and if necessary, expansion of your existing business. Growth plans focus on marketing, sales, operations, and production not often covered in depth in business plans. These details are important to investors and bankers when based on reliable information and clear metrics, which often presents more of a challenge for startups.

Growth plans are best when focused on a single opportunity or two if the two are closely related. If you have multiple lines of business, you may find you need multiple growth plans. This is true even if some of the sections in each plan are exactly the same.

Characteristics of a Good Plan

Make sure your plan covers all of your bases. A good plan considers:

- Business Story
- High-Level Strategies
- Business Baseline
- Key Metrics
- Cost of Success
- Timelines
- Risks

Business Story. Often, the motivation behind success, enticing investors, and intriguing loan officers is the story behind your business and your business opportunity. A good plan does not start at what you do. It begins with who the business is and why it exists. A good business story connects the reader on an emotional level.

Your business story includes your mission, vision, and values. Well-written plans have the reader cheering for your success. Make sure each stage of the plan tells a little more of your story.

High-Level Strategies. Plans document the key strategies important to building your business opportunity which must include your timeline, marketing, sales, and pricing. Growth plans tend to go into much more detail about strategies than business plans.

Cost of Success. New expenses in terms of staffing, planning, equipment, and space necessary to create a stable foundation often closely follow success. An adequate investment in equipment and maintenance helps prevent breakdowns and costly repairs. An appropriate investment in resources avoids overworking team members. Proper supervision and support of your team members needed to succeed may require growing your management team. Include the cost of success in your plan from the very beginning to ensure you have the budget to grow.

Business Baseline. No plan is a plan without a starting point. Your starting point is a baseline. Set a baseline so that when course corrections are necessary each change can be carefully thought through. Use performance metrics against the baseline to provide more accurate measurements of success.

Key Metrics. Metrics in a plan set up checks and balances that help make sure that the plan is realistic. Achievable timelines, realistic financial ratios, predictable growth rate numbers, and so on help you make important business decisions. Businesses that have been around for a while have history to help make these types of predictions. Startups often must do more research to find the data necessary.

Startups can often use data from existing competitors. Take time to find useful predictive data. Taking time to be accurate reduces risk. The more transparent your data is to everyone taking a risk, the better.

Timelines. Understanding how long it takes to begin to make money is important. Without a timeline, you cannot know for sure. Every opportunity creates expenses that require investment. The investment may be coming from inside your company, your personal funds, or from outside through loans, grants, or money from investors.

For example, if your opportunity means that you must increase staff and add new managers and supervisors you want to plan for that. If you must purchase new equipment to deliver your goods or services to new customers that comes at a price as well. The investment may be coming from inside your company, your personal funds, or from outside through loans, grants, or money from investors.

Outside investors want to make money on their investments. Before accepting money, make sure that your investor(s) understand the amount of time you predict it will take for the investment to net a positive return. The best policy is to under promise and over deliver.

Avoid borrowing too quickly, making sure to time debt so the weight of the payments is not too large for the business to manage until new income covers the cost. Remember your pricing must cover your new costs before you deplete your investment dollars. Timing debt helps provide the infrastructure you need for success while still meeting your predicted profit margins when done right.

Risks. Pointing out risks in your plan may seem counterintuitive However, investors want to know that you understand what you are up against. A short list of your 5 to 10 biggest risks is often enough to prove you understand your business.

Strategies for Success

Align your key strategies centered around your opportunity with your mission, vision, and values. A strategy is essentially a long-term plan that provides the direction necessary to achieve a goal or set of goals over a period of time. Multiple focused strategic plans often strive toward the same outcome.

Planning is similar at all levels of business. Many of the steps are the same whether you are creating a business plan, a growth plan, a strategic plan, or a project plan. The skills you develop writing your first plan help you build any other plans you need to support the success of your business. If you begin planning early, you will likely soon discover strategic plans provide the information you need to make even the most important business decisions.

Often, you may be tempted to dive in with little or no planning at all. Many entrepreneurs do. German philosopher Arthur Schopenhauer proposed that "talent achieves what others cannot achieve, whereas genius achieves what others cannot imagine" in his book, *The Word as Will and Representation*. (Schopenhauer 2010) Many entrepreneurs agree. However, a good plan takes the talents necessary to implement a genius idea and turns it into a reality which is the cornerstone of success.

Lots of brilliant entrepreneurs start businesses that are born of great, even genius ideas. Only some of them succeed. A study in the *Journal of Business Venturing* found that planning does indeed improve small business performance for both startups and ongoing ventures that use a process for writing plans. It suggests that as businesses gain experience and skill in planning the benefit increases. The study advocates for continued planning no matter how long your business has been around, reporting that robust organized planning for growth increases success.

However, this same study cautions against an informal approach. "Since business planning in new and established small firms is oftentimes informal, iterative, incremental, unstructured, and irregular leading to no written outcome, the development of these firms might suffer. Our findings caution practitioners to avoid these frequent shortcomings of business planning and apply both formal and more sophisticated planning approaches."

Source (Brinckmann 2017)

Strategic Goals

Goals set the direction and momentum of any business and are key to expanding capacity. Businesses without goals tend to lack direction. The most successful businesses meet goals. Make your goals part of your every-day operations. Do not let your goals become a list you never look at once written. Act in an organized manner to do the steps necessary for success such as those laid out for you in the Roadmap for Success.

While your goals may be listed in your business or growth plan for three, five, or ten years, you may need to break them down further. This is where the Roadmap to Success single-year plan becomes important. Use the one-year plan to break down your larger goals into achievable segments that can be clearly measured.

Strategic plans centered around your goals are essential to making sure your opportunity becomes a success. Well-written plans built around an opportunity often include details about each.

Types of Strategic Plans

Strategies may include:

- Time
- Marketing
- Pricing
- Sales

Time Strategy. Your time strategy is a piece of the overall strategic plan that focuses on when. Timelines such as roadmaps, project plans, development plans, and delivery schedules make up your time strategy. Your time strategy may be your MOST crucial element of success because it sets timelines and deadlines.

Timelines are not just estimates of the time it takes to do tasks. Timelines set goals measured by milestones that move your efforts forward. Deadlines create accountability by helping you and your team focus the energy and efforts necessary to achieve a goal. Your timeline creates an urgency to move forward.

Take time now to build the timelines important to your success. Begin with your building a roadmap for your opportunity. Add any other timelines crucial to your success.

Marketing Strategy. Your marketing strategy is best described as your overall game plan for reaching prospective consumers and leading them down the path to becoming buyers. This path is often called a channel. Deciding if a market exists is not the same as creating a market strategy. Clearly, the market must be big enough to allow you to attract your share of the right customers who are your potential buyers. That share of potential buyers must be big enough for you to make a profit. Your market strategy connects you to those buyers in a channel.

Develop your marketing strategy by gathering the information you need. Building a strategy requires you to define your:

- Channel(s)
- Size
- Volume
- Value

Channels

Channels build connections or paths from the provider of goods and/or services to the purchaser. Most businesses have more than one path to a customer. However, channels are not necessarily equally profitable. You may soon discover you do not have the budget to follow each path. You must prioritize. The more you understand about each channel, the easier prioritizing your path becomes.

What you have to offer becomes viable only when you understand how to reach your potential buyer. All channel paths eventually lead to a decision-making buyer. However, there may twists and turns along the way. Corporate decisions may come through procurement but then have to be approved by the ultimate user, their management, and in some cases the company's legal counsel. Sometimes the ultimate user goes through management to make a procurement request. Children may ask parents. Parents may decide for their children who are never asked before being given your product or taking advantage of your service.

The most complicated path is when a service is contracted by a decision-making buyer, but the customer makes the final purchasing choice.

Sometimes the needs and wants of the decision maker do not align with the needs and wants of the customer. Being clear which needs and wants must be met can be key to success. When you take a moment to consider the path to a willing and able decision-making buyer, you are better at making decisions about any proposed opportunity.

For example, businesses that produce products often compete for shelf space in brick and mortar stores. Entrepreneurs often cannot reach the person who actually uses the product until a corporate store buyer gives them shelf space. Businesses that market to children know that parents make the final buying decision. Adult children may make decisions for elderly parents.

For instance, a phone and video calling service provider for the incarcerated has channels that are complex. Initial contracts come from B2G and B2C agreements. Actual purchases come from a very targeted B2C market. To make matters more difficult, the needs and wants of the B2G and B2C markets are often diametrically opposed to those of the B2C purchasers. There is no way to reach the B2C purchasers without a B2G or B2C agreement.

As it turns out, those who run jail and prison facilities do not want those they house to have access to uncontrolled calls, videos, and chats. These leaders know uncontrolled communications increase violence and crime. Still inmates have the need and the right to communicate with their lawyers, family, colleagues, and friends. Jails and prisons must make those conversations possible to be compliant with regulations and laws. The needs are clear.

The wants are however very different. Facility leaders want to avoid violence and crime while supporting law enforcement in getting and maintaining convictions. They want the heavy costs of security features to be covered by the company that provides these services. Consumers want clear private connections with the outside world reducing the risk of conviction and sometimes increasing the probability of success on appeal. Their wants could not be more different.

To make things more complicated often, the consumer who pays for the call is a friend or family member who has a set of wants of their own. They want the calls to be inexpensive. In addition, they want the minutes to be easy to buy, calls and video connections easy to make, and the connections to be clear. They may have other wants as well. Even the user and the purchaser can have different wants.

At each stage of the path, a different marketing channel is necessary. Your path is likely much simpler. Your path may include only one or many buyer profiles. Keep in mind, each buyer profile may follow more than one channel path. Understanding the path(s) is important.

Understanding your channels requires understanding the following:

- Decision Making
- Barriers
- Loyalty
- Patterns
- Priorities

Decisions

After looking at who the decision-making buyer is, it becomes clear to see the purchaser is not always the user of your goods or services. While B2C customers may make personal decisions with little or no input, B2B and B2G buyers may need a great deal of input. Your initial contact may not even be the decision maker. Understanding how to determine who the decision maker(s) are and how to get to them is key to defining a marketing path.

Barriers

Consider your paths to willing and able decision-making buyers and determine if there are barriers in your way. If the paths are clear then you may find a decision to move forward is easy. If barriers exist, you may want to do more research. Do any necessary research to determine how difficult, costly, or complex removing each barrier might be.

Barriers add risks, cost money, and increase the time it takes to be successful. Do not move forward if you have not found a path over, under, around, or through your barrier. It is far less costly to decide not to pursue a blocked path at this stage than it is after you have spent more time and money on your opportunity.

Discovering a barrier is not necessarily the end. Assess every barrier separately. Consider the cost to remove the block in both dollars and time. Be sure that everyone appropriate on your team gets a chance to give feedback. Make sure everyone impacted is aware.

Loyalty

A lot gets said about brand loyalty and that can be confusing. Loyalty comes in many forms. For some, it means that buyers do purchase multiple products or services in your brand because they admire and/ or trust that your brand delivers. For others, loyalty means repeat purchases of a single product or service. For still others, loyalty means that satisfied customers recommend your goods or services to other potential customers.

Understanding what makes your potential customer turn into a willing and able repeat buyer or a brand ambassador offering regular recommendations builds repeatable revenue. Loyalty creates the credibility necessary for sustained growth. Often, businesses see a bump in loyalty returns at predictable intervals. Businesses that have done well for 3, 5, and 10 years years regularly frequently report seeing an increase in referrals and repeat revenue from regular customers.

Patterns

Purchasing patterns are more than just the habits of your buyer. They are the predictable repeatable actions you identified in channels and buyer profiles. Understanding these patterns allows you to identify your most efficient and effective marketing channels and the actions necessary to entice your buyers.

These patterns are often influenced by many of these factors:

- Ease of Purchase
- Perishability
- Availability
- Reliable Expectations
- Season
- Economic Upturns or Downturns
- Preferences
- Employer Purchasing Rules
- Recommendations
- Sales Influencers
- Goals and Motivations
- Price

Priorities

Customers have budgets. When budgets get tight customers must often decide between competing needs. Understanding where your goods and/or services fall in priority for your customers prepares you for shifts in the market. You may want to set aside a bigger reserve of earnings when you know that your business is rated higher as a wanted product and/or service and lower as a needed product and/or service.

For example, when the economy gets tight, many start to consider the difference between a need and a want more carefully. Companies frequently put off training, incentive purchases, and motivational activities in favor of making payroll when times are tougher. Consumers often forego big ticket purchases of luxury items during lean times as well. Even government purchases and payments often become delayed or may be put on hold as legislators deal with budget shortfalls.

Go/No Go Decision

Consider these questions after defining your market:

- Are there regulations or laws that shrink your market?
- Is the market of willing and able buyers for your opportunity big enough to make your opportunity worth the risk and expense of moving forward?
- Are there economic barriers that may impact your timing?

Determine if you should move forward.

Yes. If yes, then you are ready to move ahead and consider what channels best serve your market.

No. If no, then this is not the right time to move forward.

Maybe. Consider what changes and revisions you could make to your product or service that would overcome these obstacles. Measure the cost, effort, and time it would take to change the regulations or laws that block your success to determine if moving forward is still a possibility.

Identifying Channels

No path is wrong when the path is accurate. It may look like:

- Social media, to click ad, to website, to SaaS purchase
- In-store shopping, to sales counter, to purchase
- Online review by company users, to answer, to contact from lead, to review by legal representatives and/or auditors, to drafting, to signing a contract

Here are some examples of channels often used:

Blogs	Publicity	PR (conventional)
Offline Ads	Content	E-mail
Word of Mouth (Viral)	Engineered Tools	Business Development
Sales	Affiliate Marketing	Partner Platforms
Tradeshows	Networking Events	Speaking Engagements
Community Building	Advice	Organic Growth

Few small businesses use every channel available. Success depends upon picking a channel that is not only the best for your product or service, but is also something your team is likely to do without procrastination. These become your priorities. Most small businesses do best if they select no more than three channels.

Step One—Select Channels

Select channels by following the steps below:

1. Take a look at the list of marketing channel opportunities and then add any others that you can think of that would be effective for you.
2. Make a copy of your list so you have a duplicate version.
3. List the channels you might use.
4. Review the list and number the listed opportunities from most effective to least effective starting with one.

5. Use the duplicate list of channels that you created earlier to rank the channel opportunities from lowest to highest based on activities you or your team are likely to do without procrastination.

6. Compare the lists and determine which three channels are the highest on both lists.

Step Two—Prioritize Channels

Select one to three effective channels that are also highest on your list of channels that contain things you or your team are most likely to be willing to do.

Note that some experts say that in the early stage of the business you should select just one and only add to your list as you become successful and effective at using your first choice. This may be true if you have little time for marketing. If you do not have anyone on your team to actively market without procrastination, then it will not matter how effective the channel is for you. Marketing will not work if the effort never happens because no one does it. It pays to focus on the strategies that are both effective and likely. Likely strategies are those that your team is most likely to do continuously without procrastination.

Step Three—Define Marketing Channel Options

Consider each of the channels you selected. Create a chart with a column for each channel. List the various marketing options for each channel in the appropriate column (Table 6.3). The lists do not have to be long. They should be complete. If the list gets so long it begins to look like too much, then prioritize the list so that you can build a plan to get it all done over time.

It will look something like this (Table 6.4):

Table 6.3 Channels

Channel 1	Channel 2	Channel 3

Table 6.4 Channel Tasks

Online	National Networking	Publications
Set up Facebook Group Create LinkedIn Page Start Instagram Account Set up Twitter account Build Website Create Short YouTube Videos and place on all social media Publish articles on popular websites Add content to each social media account weekly	Speaking Engagements Speak on Panels Offer on topic trainings to groups of potential customers	Write a book Publish the book Make the book available to college students

Step Four—Define Channel Paths

1. Take a moment to meet with your team.
2. Consider each path to a decision.
3. Draw the pathway so that everyone can see it.

Drawing each path often helps identify twists and turns. It may even help you discover new paths you have not previously considered. Understanding your channel paths provides the information necessary to build successful marketing campaigns.

Testing Your Channels

You want to make sure the assumptions you made about your channels are correct before you spend your budget and your time. It pays to be sure your path actually reaches your target market of willing and able buyers. The theory behind testing is that if you can reach a few targeted buyers with a little effort, then you can increase your effort and reach even more. Use what you learn about your buyers real wants and needs in testing to tweak your campaigns and improve your ability to connect.

Here are some tests to consider:

- Customer/User Experience
- Focus Groups
- Experimentation
- Events

Customer/User Experience

If buying or using your product or service is difficult, you can be assured that there is a hidden opportunity. Grow your market by solving the problem or improving the customer experience or let your competitor benefit at your expense. Customer/user experience testing uncovers what buying and/or using your product or benefiting from your service is like for your customers. This testing allows you to make improvements regarding how you market, deliver, or produce your product and/or service to increase your customer's satisfaction. Clearly, to do that, you must know what is important to your customer.

A good example of growing market share through improving the customer experience starts with WordPerfect. Unless you are over 50, it is unlikely you even recognized the name. WordPerfect went on the market as one of the first computerized word processing tools available to the general public. It was the first time a user could correct work without retyping or using messy correction fluid. It was wildly popular and soon made typewriters that had been an office staple for 100 years obsolete. The secret of WordPerfect's success was improving the user experience of typists.

However, to use WordPerfect, the user had to learn a long series of computer commands that took some time to master. Just when WordPerfect was celebrating a decade of dominance in the market along came Apple. Their Macintosh software was easy to use and took almost no time to learn. They thought the secret of their success was better computers. It was actually improving the user experience for those who were willing to pay more for ease of use. Apple quickly stole 30 percent of the word processing market; however, the less-expensive WordPerfect was still dominant.

Then along came Microsoft Office signaling the end of WordPerfect. It would run on far-less expensive computers. Word soon became the preferred word processing tool capturing 80 percent of the market. Microsoft understood that they were selling was a better user experience and not better computers.

Focus Groups

It pays to ask your customers what they need and how they want to get it. Even if your business is doing well, understanding your customers is a good idea. Sometimes business owners fall into a growing market where they think they are providing one thing, but they are actually meeting the need for something else. Truly understanding what about your product or service meets your needs will help protect you from market changes.

Ernest Dichter PhD pioneered the idea of reaching out to groups of users who best represent a profile of buyers to ask what they wanted and why. He used carefully planned questions to uncover what group members really wanted. The purpose was to better focus a business on customers' real motivations. (Schwarzkopf 2010)

To understand why focus groups are so useful, look back at the very beginning to the boxed cake industry. According to *Bon Appetite* writer Michael Y. Park, 1940s flour mills jumped into the cake market after World War II soldiers returned home. Supplies that had been in short supply because of the war were suddenly widely available again along with the workforce to create them and more people to buy them.

Cake sales plummeted in the 1950s. Box cake manufacturers were confused. Along came Ernest Dichter with a plan to find out why. Clearly, what customers wanted had mysteriously changed. They were still delivering convenience and savings with a tasty treat in a box, but it was not enough.

Ernest Dichter returned from his focus groups with the news that bakers wanted to be more involved in the process. He asking bakers to add a few ingredients. He theorized that bakers would feel more a part of their creation if they contributed to the mix themselves. However, while he was right about the motivation, he may have been wrong about the answer.

According to Park, he was right but for the wrong reason. Buyers wanted creativity. Can frosting was the answer, "Box covers, recipes, and home-making magazines showcased elaborate cake constructions that looked like miniature football fields, or European castles, or three-ring circuses. A partner product saved the industry." (Park 2013)

Park's story shows that focus group information must be carefully digested and tested to be sure that the interpretation of the information best serves the needs of your business. You can see from the history of box cakes that the market shifted. Yet, what looked like a looming disaster became another opportunity. Boxed cake companies began to create canned frosting as a partner product to make creative masterpieces even easier for home bakers and generated even more revenue.

Create a Focus Group

Follow the steps below to create a focus group:

Step One—Make Preparations

1. Determine your sample size or how many people to include.
2. Identify the demographics that best represent your target customer such as gender, age, income range, and so on.
3. Select your topic.
4. Develop a concise list of open-ended questions taking care to stay on topic.
5. Create consent and feedback forms.
6. Determine how long the focus group must last to cover each of your questions taking care to stay within two hours.
   Note Typical discussions tend to run 10 minutes per question.
7. Select a gathering venue, date, and time.
8. Gather supplies such as name tags, gift cards, swag bags, recording equipment, and sound equipment as necessary.
9. Invite target participants who match the demographic identified earlier. Invite 1/3 more participants than you decided to include to account for those who do not come after confirming.

Step Two—Prepare for the Day

1. Make the room comfortable and inviting.
2. Arrange chairs so everyone can be heard and be comfortable.
3. Make sure lighting is appropriate for reading the consent forms.
4. Set up any recording equipment or sound equipment as necessary.
5. Put out a sign in form to confirm the participant's names.
6. Put name tags and markers out where they are easy to access.

Step Three—Host the Focus Group

1. Greet guests as they arrive, ask them to make a name tag, and give them the consent form to review and sign.
2. Gather the consent forms.
3. Introduce yourself, the facilitator, and your team.

4. Walk participants through an ice breaker game to increase their comfort with each other.

5. Set ground rules for respect.

6. Ask questions and record the answers making sure everyone gets a turn to speak regularly.

7. Hand out feedback forms and ask that the participants each complete one before leaving.

8. Thank everyone for coming and give them any promised reward. Note→Provide some reward for their time even if none was promised.

Step Four—Use Your Results

1. Create a transcript of the event from the recording.

2. Review the transcript with appropriate members of your team.

3. Document your findings.

4. Use your findings to update your strategies.

Experimentation

Use marketing channel experiments to validate theories before making big investments. Proper testing requires skills in test procedures, data science, and data analytics and may be best left to the experts. The only exception may be simple digital traffic experiments.

Most browsers such as Google, Firefox, or Bing provide digital analytics that have been validated by other users and tend to produce reliable results. Make sure you are comfortable relying on the data before investing your time and money. Additionally, there are a wide range of free and low-cost tools available on the Internet to test digital marketing channels that provide a greater level of detail.

Events

Use networking gatherings, conferences, annual association meetings, workshops, and so on to gain exposure to your target market. Events may be in person, virtual, or a combination of both. Your presence at in person events may require serving as a guest speaker, hosting a booth, sponsoring WIFI, providing exhibits, or as a sponsor. Events can be the key to taking off. According to business writer Nick Douglas, "Twitter put TVs in the lobbies and hallways of the SXSW (South by Southwest) conference in 2007, showing live feeds of tweets from the event. Of course everyone wanted to see their own tweet on screen, and as a result, their traffic ballooned from 20,000 to 60,000 tweets per day during the event." (Douglas 2007)

Marketing Campaigns

Once you know what your end goal is and which one to three channels are most likely to work for you, begin building your market strategy. For example, if local networking is the best channel for you, join your chamber of commerce and/or a networking group. Your money is better spent than it would be to buy social media ads. However, if your best channel is online marketing, social media ads become an important part of your strategy. Your strategy must incorporate the best way to meet your potential customers for your channel.

Many people confuse marketing campaigns with sales pitches. Recognizing the difference increases the effectiveness of your campaign. If you think of a channel as a path, then a marketing campaign is the vehicle that moves your sales pitch in front of a potential buyer. Your channel path must be correct and your campaign vehicle successful BEFORE your customer ever gets to see or hear your sales pitch. Matching the right campaign to the most effective channel is essential.

There are many campaigns that move buyers through the channels you selected. Here are a few often-used campaigns to consider:

Always start with putting a well-thought-out campaign plan in writing. Writing your plan provide clarity. Consider the time and resources necessary to carry out your campaign. Determine your goals and set metrics to measure your success.

Direct Mail	Conference Follow-up	Referral Follow-up
E-mail	Trade Show Booths	Social Media Engagement
Networking	Sales Calls	Business Community Engagement
In person presentations	Advice Response	Conventional Public Relations
Web Contact Follow-up	Advertising	Search Engine Optimization (SEO)

Some campaigns are short and easily monitored. Others are long and need a plan with metric milestones reviewed regularly in a spreadsheet or better yet in your Customer Relationship Management (CRM) application to stay on track. Use metrics to help you understand your sales cycle. Review your predictions against what actually happens so you plan better next time. These efforts lead to better sales forecasts. Not only that, but your accumulated data provides the stats that help you determine what campaigns work best for each of your channels.

Customer Base

Calculate your customer base by determining the number of willing and able buyers that make up your market share per channel. Your share determines the size of your market. Your market size is determined by buyer profiles, targeted by prioritized channels to reach buyers by campaigns.

Size matters in both number of customers that make up your customer base in your channel and the market share they represent. It is easy to understand that once you identify the subset of buyers who are willing and able to buy, the market must be big enough to accommodate both you and your competitors. It is rare that someone dominates any given market. It happens when a patented product is so innovative competitors cannot figure out a way into the market. Use realistic numbers when determining your likely portion of the market.

Statistics to determine the size of your market are often easy to find if you know where and how to look. Here are some options:

- Market Analysis Software
- Market Consultants
- Industry Reports
- Market Publications
- Government Research
    - Department of Commerce
    - U.S. Census Bureau's Annual Surveys
    - Federal Trade Commission Studies
    - Department of Treasury
    - SBA

- SBA and Accelerator Business Advisors (often free)
- Trade Associations
- U.S. Chamber of Commerce

Buyer Research. Buyers you cannot or will not reach are not part of your target. When researching your market to build a cohesive market strategy for your channel, consider:

- Geographical Region
- Familiarity
- Stability
- Penetration
- Volume
- Value

Geographical Region

Make sure to measure your share of the market only against your real customers. A local business addresses only local customers' needs, only considers the local market and not every customer in the United States. An online merchant must consider everyone online. A national service must consider the market for the entire country.

Familiarity

The more familiar your product or services is, the more you must work to stand out in the crowd to gain market share. Everyone knows what services are offered by a plumber, doctor, attorney, and so on, making it important to determine what makes your product/service different than your competitors. Think about your opportunity statement and about what makes your product and/or service better, unique, and/or more valuable. Determine how best to use that to get your potential customers' attention.

Very innovative products and services, on the other hand, may require some education for the consumer. It may take some time and effort to convince your customers they have a need. Cars were called horseless carriages to help consumers relate the auto to their current needs. Home computers did not catch on until enough of the public was familiar with desktops at work 185 years after the first computer was marketed.

The first computer was a punch card loom that revolutionized the textile industry in 1801. Later, Thomas Watson Jr. of IBM led the effort to build the computer as we know it today. It could calculate 26 complex equations at one time using the first computer language developed by Grace Hopper in the early 1950s. IBM determined their market to be very large governments and priced their computing machine to make a profit if they sold three. Clearly, they underestimated this life-changing innovation. (Mann 2015)

Trend products, on the other hand, can take market share overnight and be gone a year later such as iPods. Others become part of the culture like water bottles, but competition soon causes many competitors that steal market share. If you are investing in a trendy idea as your next opportunity, plan for a short profitable market life cycle.

It is important to know which category your product and/or service belongs. Accurate predictions help you create a viable strategy. If you are changing the world, it may take some time. Plan for that.

Penetration

Determine market penetration by how much of your target market you have or you will need to capture. Your penetration is the percentage of business you capture compared against the entire market in your channel. For example, in the early days IBM captured 100 percent of the super computing market. It was the innovator. Since then, competitors have greatly reduced IBMs dominance and penetration. Today IBM struggles to stay in the top 10. You need enough market share to stay competitive. Competitive resilience comes from being able to capture enough of the market so that your competitors do not overwhelm you. (Shankand 2004)

Stability

Stability comes from having enough customers so that the loss of one does not create a risk of failure. Small businesses owners and leaders that rely heavily on too few customers find their business in peril if just one relationship ends. A group of researchers reported that companies with a broad customer base who do not rely too heavily on one or two key customers are more likely to succeed. In a study called *A knowledge-based view of managing dependence on a key customer*, "The study found a significant negative impact of key customer dependence on firm survival." (Yli-Renko, Deno, and Janakiraman 2020)

What this means is that winning that one big customer may get you started but wise entrepreneurs do not stop there. Every business needs a stability percentage. Your stability percentage indicates the highest percentage of business that can be provided by one buyer relationship. Determine your stability percentage by considering how much business you can lose and still survive.

Typically, avoid having any one customer provide more than 30 percent of your business. Buyers in this case also include distributors. For example, if you sell through one big box chain only, you may have a popular product with 1,000s of customers, but you have only one buyer relationship. If that goes away then reaching your customers becomes problematic overnight.

Volume

The volume of your market is defined as the number of products or services you sell divided by the number available for purchase in the market at any price. Many people assume that high volume equals high profits. This is not necessarily true. If you discount your products or services to capture volume, sometimes that means your profit margin suffers. Avoid getting work that creates negative revenue.

Market Volume = Market Size × Penetration Rate (#Sold/Projected Sales)

Value

Once you understand your market volume, you can use your volume and price to determine the value of your market. Determine the monetary value of your market share to decide if there is a profit margin worth pursuing. Knowing your market value is key to determining if an opportunity is worth the investment and effort it takes to make it successful. If you find that you would not make a profit even if you captured 90 percent of the market volume, then you know your opportunity cannot support your business. However, if just 2 percent meets your financial goals then the market value suggests a promising opportunity exists.

Market Value = Market Volume × Average Market Price

Pricing Strategy

The price you want to set for your goods and services cannot be more than a willing buyer is both able and willing to pay. Able is as important as willing. Many B2B and B2G entities have made the mistake of creating products or developing services their customers wanted but were prevented from buying because of budgetary restraints, regulations, or other contract agreements that make the price their customers could pay less than the price that was acceptable. The customers might have been willing. They just were not able to complete the deal.

Common pricing strategies include:

- Competitive
- Cost Plus
- Demand-Based
- Mixed

Competitive. Competitive pricing considers what others in the marketplace charge for like goods or services. Your Competitor Evaluation provides insights into competitor pricing that sets a maximum and a minimum for the goods or services in your channel. Keep in mind that different channels may pay different prices for the same goods or services.

For example, luxury buyers pay more when convinced they are getting something exclusive, special, or better than the average buyer can afford. This is the reason a car buyer pays more for a Mercedes than for a Ford. Both are cars, but the channels are different. Mercedes asks higher prices for their vehicles because they built a reputation of using only the best parts. Their 21st century slogan "the best or nothing" reminds their buyers of why they should want to pay more.

It is clear to see that it pays to understand the customers in each channel so that you price appropriately. If you price too low, your customers may not trust that your goods or services are as good as your competitors. If you price too high, your customers may think you do not understand your market or your competitor's product or service is a better value.

Consider using discount pricing to get the attention of your customers. Done right, you can continue to increase your prices as your goods or services become more in demand. Take care though because if done wrong you end up with buyers who are not able or are not willing to pay a fair price and so turn to you only as a last resort.

Cost Plus. Cost plus pricing sets a margin over cost used to ensure profitability. You see this pricing frequently in retail where goods are bought from manufacturers or distributors and sold to consumers at a marked-up price. Cost plus is often used in industries such as commodities where costs change rapidly as well. Additionally, cost plus may be used successfully for services in high demand that have few competitors. Service firms often use cost plus to charge for services provided to be sure they make a profit above overhead on the services their resources provide too.

Demand-Based. Demand-based pricing works for goods or services in short supply when your customer is willing to pay a premium. Customers may be collectors or early adopters. They might also need services that are in high demand when there are few resources with the desire or skills to deliver.

Consider the Great Resignation of 2021 when companies reached out to reclaim resources who had been released during the Covid-19 pandemic only to find many did not want to return. Wages and contract payments went up as jobs became harder to fill. Companies began paying signing bonuses, improving benefits, and negotiating working conditions to attract the labor they needed to be successful.

Prices went up across all industries in 2021 according to the U.S. Bureau of Labor Statistics as well because supply chains bogged down making getting products and the pieces and parts to make products across borders difficult. Car prices rose 35 percent. Gas went up to a 10 year high. Companies across the board began raising pricing to accommodate increased costs for labor and materials. (U.S. Bureau of Labor Statistics 2021)

Demand-based pricing is not fixed. When demand is high, so is the price. When demand wanes, prices go down as well. Entrepreneurs who depend on early adopters must understand when that market has been saturated in time to make the discounts necessary to stay viable. Even the most intriguing innovations do not stay new forever.

Mixed. Oftentimes, the best pricing strategy is built based on a combination of the three most common strategies that works for you. Demand always has an impact. As markets shift and customers change, the best pricing strategies are determined by what works in the moment.

Go/No Go Decision

Once you have all the information, meet with your team and decide whether to go forward or vote No Go and look for another opportunity. Determine if there is a market with a target share big enough to meet your end goal. Determining if what you have to offer is exactly what your customers want is a part of that. If your first opportunity is a No Go that does not mean you are done. It just means you have not found the right opportunity.

Yes. If yes. then move forward with confidence.

No. If no, this is not the time to move forward.

Maybe. Consider whether there are ways to expand your market. There are only a few options:

- Increase the size of your market
- Raise the price of your product or service high enough to make a profit
- Change your opportunity so that more people will be willing to make a purchase at your price

- Convert buyers who are able but not willing to buy
- Abandon your opportunity before spending more time and money

Sales Strategy

Once you understand your market position craft a strategic sales plan that is in alignment with your company's mission, vision, and values. Use the clarity gained from researching your market to create a plan that more accurately targets the right industries, audiences, and customers. For every channel worth pursuing, there is a way to get the attention of your customers. Your market strategy gets the attention. Use your sales strategy to close the deal. Your plan becomes the hub around which you build the path to sales success.

Sales Plan. Many people get confused by the difference between a marketing plan and a sales plan. Many think they are the same thing. They are not. Marketing makes your potential customers aware of your services or product. Sales coverts those potential customers into buyers.

All businesses no matter how small, have a pathway to a sale. Some are shorter than others. The length of time it takes to convert a potential customer to a buyer is called lead time. Lead time can be minutes or months. A restaurant turns a customer into a buyer in minutes. An engineering company may bid for a job and not know if they have been selected for months. The important thing is to understand your funnel and be able to plan to cover your costs until that sale is made.

The steps to build your sales funnel and then move forward are different than the steps to market in your market channel.

A good sales plan includes at the minimum:

- Goals
- Funnel(s)
- Resources
- Action Plans
- Processes

- Budgets
- Exposure
- Tracking
- Refinements

Sales Goals

Your sales goals are the KPIs you set for your sales efforts. Setting clear achievable goals is a process. No company can succeed without eventually earning a profit. Sales goals are about numbers. Start by determining how much money your company must make to cover the expenses your opportunity creates and then turn the desired profit. Your profit goal must be clear even if you know you will not reach it in your first year.

Many new opportunities require a period of investment that means operating at a loss in the beginning. It took Amazon founder Jeff Bezos seven years to become profitable. Without a clear and realistic strategic sales plan with realistic goals, he would not have ever become the richest man in the United States multiple years running. Goals set his plan in motion.

Use your desired revenue to determine the volume of sales necessary to achieve your goals and meet your KPIs, then work backward. Use these goals to quantify the work that has to be done at each stage of your funnel to reach success. Break your goals down into increments and measure them monthly, quarterly, and annually to make sure you are on target.

For example, if you want to a make $100,000 profit over a year on your opportunity and the expense to produce your goods and/or services are 50 percent then you must make $2000,000 to meet your revenue goals. You may plan to do that by making $35,000 in the first quarter, $45,000 in the second quarter, $50,000 in the third quarter, and $70,000 in the last quarter. Your monthly revenue goals are determined by what you expect to earn each quarter.

Sales Funnels

Few people become customers spontaneously. Most customers follow a path regardless of whether they are consumers, corporate buyers, or government procurement specialists. The path can take minutes or years depending on your product or service. It begins with interest and ends

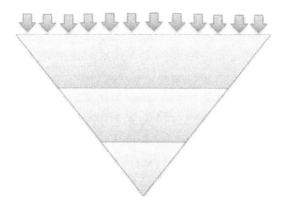

Figure 6.8 Sales Funnel

with a decision to buy. This path is called by many a sales funnel because the number of interested parties tends to drop off at each stage (Figure 6.8). You may have more than one funnel in your strategic sales plan when different funnels are necessary to reach your potential customers in each channel. Every funnel stage has a name. These names vary. The important thing is that everyone on your team knows what they mean.

Here are examples:

Leads	Prospects	Qualified	Negotiation	Sale
Lead	Contact	Interested	Sale	
Lead	Qualified	Sale		

Figure 6.9 Example sales funnel

The winnowing down of a customer pool is important. Done well, the sales funnel helps you decide where and with whom to spend your valuable time, budget, and resources (Figure 6.9). Knowing when to move on from a potential customer unlikely to buy is just as important as targeting those who will become your customers. Even if your sales cycle is very short and your price is nonnegotiable knowing what stage your potential customer is on in the buying journey helps your sales team focus on the right customers and communicate more effectively.

For example, you may know that it takes three customers to enter your store to end up with one who makes a purchase. You know browsing customers typically want less attention than someone ready to buy. You may want your sales team to quickly move from "can I help you," to "I am happy to help you with that" as soon as they recognize a decision to purchase. Regardless of your industry or how you reach your customer—in person, online, or over the phone—it is important to recognize the right moment to ask your potential customer to buy.

Funnels built on history tend to be the most accurate. If your business opportunity is new, you may want to rely on industry statistics or competitor information. Funnels let you know how many nos it takes to get one yes. Multiply those numbers by how many it takes to meet your revenue goals (Figure 6.10).

One Sale

Leads→Prospects→Qualified→Negotiation→Sale
  20   10   5   2   1

Figure 6.10 Example sales funnel one sale

Meet Revenue Goal Formula

Sales × Price = Revenue
10,000 × $100 = $1,000,000

Multiple Sales

Leads→Prospects→Qualified→Negotiation→Sale
200,000 100,000   50,000   20,000   10,000

Resources. Resources include both people necessary to carry out your plan and the tools required to be successful. The money necessary for your resource plan to work must be included in your sales plan budget. Justify the costs by the expected results. A good strategic plan ensures satisfied customers from first interest to the decision to buy again or refer you to another potential customer.

Even the best salespeople require support including salaries, bonuses, commissions, training, team-building activities, and expense accounts. Your strategic sales plan must also consider the tools available to automate sales functions and report sales progress. Many companies invest in CRM software that facilitates and automates some sales processes. Costs vary from free to as much as you want to pay. When the tools make your sales team more productive and successful, the investment is worth the cost.

Action Plan. Use an action plan to assign tasks necessary to meet your sales goals to individuals. Make sure each task has start and end dates. Tasks without deadlines tend to remain undone. An action plan is useful even if you do not have a sales staff. These plans help break down goals into achievable steps.

Reports may come from your CRM tool or from a standardized template. There are a variety of templates readily available online. You can also find one at CapacitySquared.net. Useful reports include a basic set of information such as that shown in the example below (Table 6.5):

Table 6.5 Action Plan

Channel	Task	Assigned	When	Status	Metric

Sales Processes

Regardless of the size of your team, an organized approach reinforces your strategy. Good communication and clear roles and responsibilities dictated by documented processes help make sure action plans are followed. After all, the best plan is of no use if it is never executed.

Processes must include the documented steps to success that you expect your sales team to follow. According to Debbie Mrazek, Founder of The Sales Company and Sales and Marketing Adjunct Faculty for the 10,000 Small Business, "Working with sales organizations for 25-years one thing I can tell you one of the most powerful things they can learn is how sales is a process too. Having a true sales process that can be duplicated again and again allows for success and profits from all the sales team members." (Mrazek 2021)

This does not mean that your sales processes should be carved in stone. Carefully test new processes to add to your strategy. Adding new processes over time may provide innovative ways to open new markets.

Budget. Your sales effort deserves a budget if for tracking purposes only. Small businesses often have limited resources. Budgeting and planning for what you need to meet your strategic sales plan goals only makes sense. You may track your sales budget in your overall budget or create a more detailed budget report managed by the leader of your sales department.

Getting Exposure. Consider how attendance and presence at key events may improve your bottom line. Viewing events as a sales resource in your strategic plan ensures the investment in tickets, travel, booths, and other costs are tracked as a part of your strategic plan.

Increase local exposure and credibility necessary to expand market access to your team with meaningful organization memberships. Trade and local service companies often benefit from an active chamber of commerce membership. Industry, association, mentoring, sales, and business associations and networking groups may improve sales as well when viewed as a sales resource and used strategically to boost the bottom line.

Tracking. Every plan you make to prepare your business for success must be tracked. Tracking is the only way you and your leadership team can be sure the time and money spent gets you the results you hoped for from the start. Nowhere is this more important to any entrepreneur than in sales. Make your key strategic sales plan metrics part of your company dashboard so that you are always aware of where you stand.

Making Refinements. Refining is different than inconsistently shifting from one plan to another. Refining determines how to more efficiently and effectively hit your KPIs and reach your goals. KPIs provide insights into which efforts bring the most reward because the numbers support what works and what does not. It is clear to see that you want to invest in what works and divest or make changes in those tactics that are less successful. Constant refinement is a key feature for continuous process improvement.

Holding Sales Meetings. Hold your team accountable to carrying out your sales plan. Host regular meetings even if only one person is responsible for sales. Plans may get very complicated depending on the marketing channel and the size of your business. Taking time to consider whether the plan is being carried out as expected, and how effective it is, makes sense no matter how large or small your sales force may be.

Remember marketing makes potential customers aware, but buyers are what fill your bank accounts. The time and money you spend making sure your sales plan is followed is worth the investment. Keep meetings short and to the point to encourage enthusiastic attendance. How often you have the meeting is best determined by how much work needs to be coordinated. Some businesses need meetings once a week and others only once a month. If your team is missing deadlines or team members have trouble coordinating, that is a signal suggesting you need to have meetings more often. If you have meetings and no one has anything new to report except efforts are going well then it is likely you can have meetings less often.

Sales Meeting Agenda

The agenda provides a review of efforts by each participant not to exceed three minutes asking them to answer these questions:

- What was done since the last meeting?
- What tasks are ahead or behind?
- Describe your work plan from this point to the next meeting.
- What help do you need?

If a report takes more than three minutes, it has caused a discussion you may want to take offline to keep the meeting on track.

Sales Pitch. Sometimes entrepreneurs confuse sales pitches with sales plans. The sales pitch is an element of your overall plan. While your strategy gets you to your buyer, your pitch closes the deal. For every strategy worth pursuing, there are one or more sales pitches that turn potential customers into buyers.

There are many types of pitches. Here are few of the most effective:

- Elevator Pitch Tease
- One Word Pitch

- Story Telling
- Pain Highlight
- Three Yes Answers
- Feature Superpowers
- Follow-Up
- Free Publicity

Elevator Pitch Tease

You want others to remember you and your business because they may be, or they may know the next person you want to be introduced to right now. More than that, you want those who care to ask to hear more. Good sales-people and seasoned networkers utilize a one-minute pitch often called the Elevator Pitch. Practice your pitch until it is your automatic reaction.

Elisha Otis, who invented the elevator braking system in 1852, is widely credited with the creation of the Elevator Pitch. The elevator was an innovative invention in the 1800s. Otis decided to introduce his invention to the general public at the Chicago World's Fair in 1893 by creating an open elevator platform and riding from the bottom to the top giving his elevator safety sales pitch to spectators. The idea that you could introduce yourself on the bottom floor of an elevator and say just enough to get someone's interest before the elevator arrived on the top floor was born.

People are busy. They have short attention spans made even shorter by social media. It is easy to see that getting to the point quickly in a way that encourages interest is a skill worth developing. Anyone can create an elevator pitch.

Tell people:

- Who you are.
- Who your business is.
- What makes your business valuable or unique.
- What you want.

What you want sometimes referred to as your ask which changes depending on who you are speaking to obviously. Use the following template to come up with your own pitch (Figure 6.11). Practice using the pitch with a timer until you can repeat it from start to finish in one minute without looking at any notes.

Template

I am <u>Name Here.</u>

I am the <u>Position Here</u> at <u>Business Name Here</u>

We know <u>Problem Here</u>

We offer <u>value proposition here</u>. I am proud to be a part of a company that <u>tag line here</u>

We want

- To get to know you better. May I give you my card?

- Remember me, <u>name here</u> when you need <u>products or services here.</u>

- Tell me how I can be of service to you. What would you like to know more about?

- When can we get together to talk more?

- I am looking for an investor to invest $_____ in my business

---

Figure 6.11 Elevator Pitch template

Example (Figure 6.11)

Example

I am <u>Shery Hardin.</u>

I am the <u>Co Founder of Capacity Squared</u>

We know <u>that small business owners often feel isolated and unsupported finding it difficult to locate the unique resources they need to grow like business education, part-time professionals and fractional leaders, and a way to connect with potential customers, partners, and suppliers that encourages diversity and inclusion.</u>

For this reason, we offer <u>the only social media platform designed to connect small businesses with the diverse resources, customers, partners, and suppliers they want to do business with today.</u>

I am proud to be a part of a company that <u>is building business success through community fraction-by-fraction.</u>

What You Want

- May I give you my card?
- Remember me <u>Sheryl Hardin</u> when you need <u>solutions for your small business and use this promo code IReadIt to get a discounted membership at CapacitySquared.net</u>
- Tell me how I can be of service to you. What would you like to know about building business capacity?
- When can we get together to talk more?
- I am looking for an investor to invest <u>$1,000,000</u> in my business to <u>expand our reach and grow our membership next year.</u>

Figure 6.11 Elevator Pitch example

If you think about it, everyone must be able to answer these simple questions no matter what. It is even more important for you, because you are a small business owner, a potential small business founder, or a business leader. Most often, the pitch starts out too long. Getting everything you need to say down to one minute forces you to determine what is most important about your message. Many people report that just doing the exercise of creating an Elevator Pitch brings them new clarity about their opportunity.

Fund

The ability to predict the cost of growth is essential if your small business is going to grow successfully. Rapid growth often comes with a predictable price tag. Small businesses must invest to cover the costs of startup, opportunity development, and implementation. Entrepreneurs must be able to meet the requirements of large contracts or many small contracts coming in quickly. These expenses are often upfront costs you must bare before seeing the profit that comes with the sale of goods and/or services. You must support the infrastructure that it takes to support growth. An infrastructure that is too small is like a business with a foundation that is tiny. It cannot support building and, at some point, it topples over.

There are many ways to handle the upfront costs. According to the 2021 Small Business Trends study, 59 percent of entrepreneurs funded startup and growth themselves. The study reported, "Cash is the most popular form of financing" used 39 percent of the time. The study noted another 20 percent of owners utilized 401(k) business financing often called Rollovers for Business Startups (ROBS). (SBA 2021)

Outside Funding

This means that according to the Small Business Trends study, 41 percent of entrepreneurs needed outside funding. Outside funding comes from a variety of sources. The more bankable you are, the more likely you are to be able to finance healthy growth. If after you have predicted your costs with a reliable budget you see that you need money, it is time to consider outside funding sources.

There are a number of possibilities available:

- Crowd Funding
- Grants
- Investors
- Equipment Leasing
- Loans

Crowd Funding. Crowd Funding creates a buzz for a good idea while earning money from micro investors in exchange for something of lesser value. For example, an entrepreneur might engage potential customers in funding a new solar technology to power homes by offering a smaller, less complex prototype that powers a campsite. Create or capture the interest of enthusiastic customers who spend money upfront for a variety of reasons such as:

- Those who want to have first access to a new product or new features that enhance products they already use who enjoy being early adopters
- People with expendable income who are already loyal to your brand may want to be brand ambassadors as you expand
- Social entrepreneur supporters who get satisfaction from supporting businesses that support the same causes they do
- Interested bystanders who saw your offer and found it intriguing

Grants

The U.S. Chamber of Commerce reports that at any given time there are more than 30 grant programs available to small business owners. (U.S. Chamber of Commerce 2021) Consider seeking a grant if you are up for competition and do not mind a labor-intensive process to be completed with the inherent risk of getting nothing. Every year the government, nonprofits, and corporations give out billions of dollars to small companies. Compete for grants anywhere from $5,000 up to $1,000,000 offered to deserving companies designed to benefit a specific population of businesses. Grants may be based on geography, demographics, or in most cases types of businesses.

Grant winners are often required to do detailed reporting. Grantors get their money from others. It might be donors, funds, institutions, or the government. In order to continue to offer grants programs, grant managers have to show the dollars they allocated were well spent. Most grant programs want to know they have invested well so THEY will be approved for additional funding.

Government Grants

The U.S. Chamber of Commerce has a website specifically for business grants. Per the website, grants.gov provides a database of "Federal funding opportunities published for organizations and entities supporting the development and management of government funded programs and projects." Most businesses can participate. Some opportunities require certifications. Make sure to read each grant opportunity carefully before applying. Each year, the chamber posts a list at https://buff.ly/34GYU4b. (U.S. Chamber of Commerce 2021)

Private Grants

Corporations offer grants as well. Corporation seeking to diversify their supply chain, respond to pressure from customers, or support suppliers through a time of crisis sometimes offer grants. Consider researching corporate grants when you have a relationship with the funder or when you are a match for some special program or association the corporation supports.

Nonprofit

Consider a wide variety of nonprofits when seeking grant financial support. Accelerator programs sometimes come with a cash benefit to those accepted in their programs but not always. Many foundations routinely run grant competitions annually as well. Some state—and university-supported entrepreneurial programs offer grants too.

CapacitySquared.com provides a list of recognized grant programs for your consideration. Keep in mind though that most programs choose a brief period during the year to accept applications. Others stop taking applications after the available funds are awarded without notice to the public.

Investors

Investor funding comes in many forms. Unlike grants, investors expect more than a report in return. Seek investor funding when you are willing to give up a percentage of equity in return for a round of funding. The type of round that interested investors participate in depends on the stage of your business or opportunity. You may reach out for funding in more than one round, but keep in mind that each time you do the investors expect some percentage in return.

Before seeking investor funding, be sure you know which investment round is appropriate for your business. Typical funding rounds include:

- Pre-seed
- Seed
- Series A
- Series B
- Series C

Pre-seed

Investors are interested in startups with a great idea. Often, these investors are family or friends who believe in your opportunity. However, sometimes professional investors who see a great concept may step in and provide support.

Seed

Investors in this round look for opportunities with a solid market and strong potential earnings in the very early stage of an opportunity. They may choose prospects based on growth plans or market attention. They are often called Angel Investors. These investors tend to be high net worth investors interested in startups or entrepreneurs with new opportunities. They may make a one-time investment or a series of investments over time if you meet your promised KPIs.

Series A

Investigate support from venture capitalists (VCs). These investors develop interest when you prove your concept. They may use their own money or money from an equity fund to invest in startups and entrepreneurs with great opportunities that are most often ready to launch. They especially like serial entrepreneurs with a history of success building and selling small companies. They respond to growth plans that showcase previous successes and high investor return rates.

Series B

Go after private equity firms and VCs funding small business expansion only after your proving your business model. This round is not for startups. You are suited for this round only after you have generated sales though you may not have made a profit yet. These investors may pay a higher share price than those in earlier rounds.

Series C

Consider these investors when you want to go public with an Initial Public Offering (IPO), hope to be acquired by a Special Purpose Acquisition Company (SPAC), or hope to exit by selling your successful business or business just on the verge of being successful. Use money from this round to support your new opportunity, expand market share for an existing opportunity, develop related products and/or services, or grow through acquisition.

Many times, investors target small businesses struggling in sales, financials, or operations. They target businesses without documented processes and procedures as well. They understand that while a business may be doing well now, if it does not shore up its weakest area it cannot expand capacity. An investor with success improving the weakest area may step in to buy the business at a discount to benefit from improvements that make the business more valuable.

Equipment Leases

When your new opportunity requires new hardware and equipment leasing and rent to own provides another way to cover your upfront investment. Consider leasing equipment only when you need it from short-term rental companies while work is inconsistent. Use long-term leasing when you need equipment available consistently or when short-term rentals are not an option.

Some leases require no down payment essentially funding 100 percent of the cost of the equipment. Qualifications for a lease are often much less stringent than traditional loans. Be aware however the actual cost of purchase may be much higher in a rent to own agreement than an outright purchase. Some equipment manufacturers offer lease options. Third-party leasing companies may work for you as well. These companies agree to purchase the equipment for you and then lease it back to you over time.

Loans

Debt-based financing gives you the ability to maintain full ownership of your business. There are a number of ways to finance the debt needed to expand. What you need to qualify for a loan will be different based on the organization that you turn to in order to find financing.

You must have good business and personal credit. Dunn and Bradstreet does for businesses what the personal credit reporting agencies do for people. They offer credit reports that help potential lenders and investors determine how creditworthy your organization is right now.

Bankers know large potential customers may check your Dunn and Bradstreet record before giving you that first big order for goods or services as well. Large customers want to be sure they are going to get what they ordered. If you appear to be on the verge of failure, they may choose a vendor that is more stable instead. Use a good report as a key differentiator when you go after new financing whenever possible.

Small business loans carry a higher risk than loans made to larger companies. Lenders often want to know that you as the business owner are creditworthy as well. Some may even ask for a lien against your personal collateral if your business collateral is not strong enough. Know your personal credit score from all three of the major credit reporting agencies TransUnion, Experian, and Equifax, and how that impacts your business.

Consider all types of loans available to you before deciding which is right:

- SBA government backed loans
- Community Development Financial Institutions (CDFI)
- Customers looking to ensure they have stable suppliers
- Micro loans for very small amounts most often provided by nonprofits
- Franchise loans provided by the franchiser to support new franchisees
- Merchant Cash Advance (MCA) loans paid back with a percentage of your credit card or debit card sales
- Factoring loans based on your outstanding invoices and are paid back when you get paid
- Business lines of credit are similar to credit cards in that you only pay for the credit you use
- Term loans paid out in a lump sum and must be paid back with monthly payments on the principal and interest
- Equipment loans based on the value of your assets
- Commercial real estate loans for the purchase of business property

Being Bankable

Being Bankable means being creditworthy. If you are not bankable now, then now is the time to take steps to change your credit standing. According to Deb Purvin, Senior Vice President at a national bank and Founder of the Business Owner's MBA (BOMBA), businesses that get credit tend to grow faster than those who do not. (Purvin 2021)

Bankers care about building their account portfolios. They want the bank to have plenty of account holders who want to do other business with them. Bankers want account holders who qualify for and use credit wisely. In order to meet their goals, bankers need customers who are bankable.

Watching the Five Cs of Credit

The one question a banker wants to answer is, if you are extended credit can you pay it back in the period of time you promised.

Lenders determine whether they will give you credit most often based on five factors:

- Capacity
- Conditions
- Collateral
- Capital
- Character

Capacity

This is where your opportunity-centered growth plan comes in handy. Bankers like knowing you plan for the future. They also like knowing you understand how to use debt to grow a business. If you have a line of credit, bankers like to see that you use it well.

Bankers consider how much debt you have in relation to how much credit you have today. Most lenders like to see that you are not tempted to borrow every penny possible. Make it a habit to use just about 50 percent of the credit you have available. Bankers want to know you have money you can get if something goes wrong. For this reason, it may be smart to ask for more money than you need.

Many entrepreneurs get a line of credit so that they only have to pay interest when they use the money. If you use most or even your entire line of credit to fund a new project or pay your expenses but then immediately pay the money back, bankers often believe you understand how to use debt. For this reason, it is often wise to get a line of credit before you actually need it.

Collateral

Loans are often secured by assets such as equipment, buildings, or land and are referred to as collateral. If you secure a loan with assets and default on payments, the assets may be seized to pay the debt. The value of the asset may not be determined just by its market value. Bankers often consider its liquidity and location. Assets that are easier to see and to move have more value than those that are not.

For example, a truck has less risk than a new foundation with extra support for heavy equipment. A bank may not want to but still can repossess a truck if payments are missed. It is hard to seize a foundation.

The assets do not have to belong to the business. Personal assets may be used to secure business loans as well. Many entrepreneurs use their homes, cars, and other assets as collateral. You should remember though; the bank takes back ANY asset that secured a loan no matter how personal.

Capital

Capital is defined as the overall value of all assets including physical assets such as collateral and financial assets such as cash, receivables inventory, and prepaids. Capital reduces risk. Anything that reduces the risk of default improves your chances of getting a loan. Be sure your lender knows if you can sell or collect capital to pay back debt if necessary.

Character

A good reputation begins with treating your customers, partners, and employees well. Businesses with a good reputation are more likely to succeed. Your reputation matters. Your credit history tells the story of your financial reputation. Other parts of your reputation matter as well.

If you have a history of being sued or suing others, bankers may see that as a red flag. Frequent lawsuits may indicate you have trouble living up to your obligations, contracting without conflict, or just getting along with suppliers and partners. The cost of litigation and the possibility of judgments increases risks.

As an entrepreneur, you must rely not only on the reputation of the business, but also on your personal reputation. The reputation of your team members matters as well. What others think about you may determine who does business with you. This is even more true when you have a local business in a small community. Bankers want relationships with people they would want to mingle with in other settings just like everyone else. Public intoxication, arguments, or rants on social media your banker hears about or can see do not end up on your loan application but they may impact decision making.

Conditions

The conditions of credit are the terms you agree to that include the type of loan, time to pay, and interest rate. Conditions are often dependent on credit worthiness based on the other four Cs of credit worthiness capacity, collateral, capital, character, and likelihood of success. This is why the 5Cs matter.

Bankers consider the level of risk associated with the likelihood of implementing a successful opportunity as well. It is clear to see why this would be important. However, be aware they may also consider external factors that increase risk such as the state of the economy. Periods of recession or unrest may cause bankers to assess a higher level of risk to all loans, not just yours. On the other hand, times of economic crisis may inspire government leaders to step in. During these periods of crisis, legislators often make available government-sponsored loans with generous conditions that are better than entrepreneurs might get in the best of times.

Financials Reports Bankers Love

Financial reports tell a story about your business. While this seems straight forward, sometimes it is not. Being able to show you can pay on time is what being bankable is about.

These documents are important to potential lenders:

- Cash Flow
- Balance Sheet
- Income Statement
- Budget

- Forecast
- Monthly Recurring Revenue (SaaS)

Cash Flow or Cash on Hand. There is a saying among small business owners and leaders, "Cash is king." Without cash on hand, you cannot pay your bills. Cash flow is about how much money you have on hand on any given day to meet all your financial obligations and to cover the promises you made. It includes more than cash. Liquid assets such as income, electronic funds, reserves, and sometimes credit immediately available to cover expenses count.

Collected Revenue – Cash Costs = Cash Flow

Sometimes entrepreneurs use only Cash Flow to determine financial health. Cash flow is important because forecasted profits from your opportunity are a theory to a banker. Cash on hand is a fact. Still it is only part of what you need when making a case to a banker that you are bankable.

Reserves. Reserves are to business finances what a savings account is to your personal finances. It is money set aside for promises made and to create a safety net to cover emergencies. You may not be able to maintain high cash reserves the first year of a new opportunity. In fact, you may be pulling cash from reserves instead.

Cash on Hand. Bankers know funding a new opportunity is a reasonable use of reserves. However, keep in mind that draining your reserves increases your risk. Three months is the minimum required by most banks to consider you stable. Six months to a year is even better.

Your banker may want to know the number of days you can honor your expenses with the cash that is available. This is known as Days Cash on Hand. Cash on hand may be low as a startup or while investing in your opportunity. This is no surprise. Report cash on hand using a Cash Flow Statement.

Balance Sheet. Your balance sheet is the financial history that depicts your net worth (Table 6.6). It provides a list of your current assets next to a list of your current liabilities. Bankers divide your current assets against your current liabilities to get your Current Ratio. Your current ratio represents your company's ability to make all your working capital payments (including debt payments) and so bankers want the answer to be positive.

Table 6.6 Balance Sheet

Balance Sheet			
Assets		Liabilities	
Cash	25,600	Accounts Payable	9,400
Accounts Receivable	18,125	Accrued Liabilities	12,775
Inventory	14,625	Line of Credit	25,000
Prepaids	28,200	CMLTD*	0
Current Assets	86,550	Current Liabilities	47,175

CMLTD—Current Maturities of Long-Term Debt

Current Assets/Current Liabilities = Current Ratio
86,550/47,175 = 1.83

Bankers like to see current ratio greater than 1 and in keeping with others in your same industry. Some Balance Sheets do not show a line of credit if no money has been drawn or do not break out Current Maturities of Long-Term Debt. However, these should be included as Current Liabilities when calculating the ratio. According to Deb Purvin, a banker will calculate those numbers among others any time you ask for a loan. Better to calculate them now so that you know what your banker sees. (Purvin 2021)

Income Statement. An income statement is sometimes referred to as a Profit and Loss (P and L). Many think of an income statement as a P and L because it reveals the ability of your business to generate a profit most often over a 30-day period. Use your Income Statement to provide you with the numbers necessary to calculate:

- Earnings Before Tax (EBT)
- Earnings Before Interest, Tax, Depreciation, and Amortization (EBITDA)
- Net Earnings

EBT

The profit or loss is determined by taking all revenues and subtracting all expenses from both operating and nonoperating activities to get Earning Before Tax (EBT). EBT is sometimes referred to as Pre tax Income.

Gross Profits – Total Expenses = EBT

EBITDA

Some bankers and most investors are most interested in EBITDA or Earnings Before Interest, Tax, Depreciation, and Amortization. EBITDA deducts interest, depreciation, and amortization from your earnings before tax. This is seen by many as a better reflection of Cash on Hand available to support your operations.

Net Earnings + Tax + Interest + Depreciation + Amortization = EBITDA

Net Earnings

Earnings after tax can be calculated as well to get Net Earnings after tax.

Earning Before Tax – Tax = Net Earnings

Year End Income

Year End Income statements show your income for the business year. Multiple columns can be used on one report to show multiple years. Use these reports for comparison and for making future predictions. Most often, three to five years are compared whenever possible.

Budget. Bankers and investors want to know that you understand your costs. Make a budget to estimate the total cost of your opportunity from inception to implementation. Include a detailed estimate of all costs that are likely to be incurred such as debt service, procurement, operating and labor costs, and so on.

Most financial software applications and many bank applications include a budgeting tool. Spreadsheets can be used to create a budget as well. A wide variety of budget templates are available online.

Forecast. Forecasts are created from Income Statements based on operating expense and profit projections. Forecasts are best when they reflect predictable trends supported by your industry and historical past performance. Startups do not have historical data and so must rely on realistic predictions. Make forecast predictions for each year of your business or growth plan.

Churn. A churn rate is the rate at which customers leave your business. It can be the gold standard of business health for those businesses that rely on customer loyalty for continued income. It is most important for businesses that rely on monthly fees such as insurance, SaaS, or memberships. Retail businesses such as drive-through restaurants and grocery stores often offer loyalty rewards to help better understand how often or even if customers return to better understand churn rate.

ARPU. Annual Revenue Per User (ARPU) is a key indicator of future profits or losses. Subtract renewals from churn to get ARPU.

Churn—Renewals = ARPU

SaaS Monthly Recurring Revenue. The last thing your banker may want to know if you are a SaaS provider is your Monthly Recurring Revenue (MRR). Your payment software will often figure your MRR for you. Your

MRR includes your predictable monthly revenue based on contracted payments, expected subscriptions, and annual payments recognized and posted each month. In order to calculate the MRR, you must first know your Churn rate to determine your ARPU.

MRR. Calculate MRR by multiplying the ARPU for the month by the total number of users in a given month.

ARPU × Number of Users for the Month = MRR

Credit Readiness Review

Business Advisors at SBA, SBDC, SBO regional offices, or accelerators often offer entrepreneurs credit readiness reviews. Reach out to get help as you work to understand your financials so that you become more bankable. Many are happy to do a credit review before you go before a banker. Reviews validate you are ready and that your documents are error free. The review points out gaps you may have in time to make long-term changes that improve your chances of success.

Moving From Red to Black. Your business value can only be proven by numbers. The popularity of your goods or services alone is not enough to prove the future success of your business. This does not mean that you must be making a profit right now. Many businesses go through an investment period when the business is "in the red." Bankers and investors both know that. It does mean that it must be clear that you have a plan to turn a profit.

Understanding where you are helps you know how to get where you want to be much more quickly. Consider Jeff Bezos who operated Amazon for six long years before reporting a profit in 2003. He was for a while considered to be the poster child for the dot com bubble.

However, he knew where he was headed and did not let that stop him. He would not have gotten there without a plan that included understanding his numbers. Now he is one of the richest men in the world.

Alternatives to Funding

When funding is low, give some thought to other options. Reconsider your plans looking for cost cutting measures. Consider the options below:

- Adjust the Three Key Constrains
- Build vs Buy
- Partner
- Barter

Adjust Three Key Constraints. There are three key constraints (Figure 6.12) to any business project or plan. These constraints are cost, time, and resources. If costs are a problem, consider adjusting one or both of the other two constraints. You cannot change one constraint without impacting the other two.

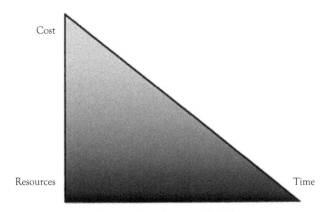

Figure 6.12 Three Key Constraints

If you want to spend less money immediately, decide where to invest because there must be a change to time or resources. There may be a change to both. It is possible that you could bring on added resources more slowly knowing that may mean it takes longer to finish. You may need to spread out major purchases such as new equipment or put off the costs of upfront marketing. Everything is a choice.

Remember resources not humans. Resources can be any number of things including technology. In the 21st century, understanding and appropriately utilizing automation may help you be successful. For this reason, there may be times when an upfront investment in automation maybe the answer to controlling time and costs in the long run.

Better understanding the parameters that control the constraints that impact decision making supports you in making better decisions. Using your budget to understand how different choices impact your plan gives you flexibility.

Build, Lease, and Buy. Use your budget and timeline when considering how choosing to build, buy, or lease changes your projected bottom line. Make a copy of your budget and your timeline and then play with your numbers. Playing is not time consuming or expensive. You may discover options you may not have considered by looking at the how the budget changes based on all your possible choices.

Consider these questions:

- Are there components of your opportunity you planned to build you can buy for less once you consider the full cost including labor and interest?
- Can you lease equipment necessary rather than buying it?
- Can you purchase refurbished or new equipment necessary to deliver and customize it to your needs rather than building from scratch?

Partner. Inviting the right partner may free up some of your budget if the partner brings equipment, tools, skill, and/or resources that you would otherwise have to budget to afford. Partners sometimes bring cash investments as well. The cost for taking on the risks and providing those resources is of course a share in the revenue in the future.

Barter. Consider what you could do for someone who could in turn help you. Bartering has been a time-honored tradition for hundreds of years though entrepreneurs often do not consider the option. Bartering for access to equipment, tools, merchandise, and/or resources available when you most need them offers a great way to stretch your budget. If you do not know other business owners that would be a good match as a barter partner, consider joining one of the many barter clubs that have sprung up since the 2008 Great Recession.

Phase Three—Execution

Execution {
Design and Prep
Document
Develop

Figure 6.13 Opportunity Development Life Cycle phase three

Design and Prep

This is the time to clarify what it takes to go from idea to reality. Make sure your design includes all the requirements necessary to deliver your product and/or service successfully. You must consider the operational system required to support your opportunity as well.

Avoid systemic issues. Part of design is making sure you have the infrastructure to support success as well. This phase (Phase 3, see Figure 6.13) works best when supported by the documentation required to think through the steps necessary for successful delivery.

Execution may take just hours or you may spend months depending on the complexity of your opportunity. However, this is the phase that best prepares your organization for success. Make sure your business is ready when you are ready to deliver.

Design. The design phase of your opportunity is where you decide how to make your opportunity meet the needs and wants of your potential customer. It is clear to see that when you are developing a new product or new use for a product you save time and money by designing it first. However, the same is true for a new service. This is the moment to decide what is a part of the service and what is not. When you are done you must know what your service entails, how you plan to deliver your service, and what a successful delivery looks like. This is the stage where you work out the kinks. Begin by creating a Requirements Checklist and a Design Document.

Requirements Checklist

Decide what success looks like. What features, functions, and services must exist and what do they have to do before you can deliver. Documenting and/or clarifying requirements necessary for success provides a safety net that helps avoid costly service gaps and design flaws. A requirements list may be as short as one page or as big as a book depending on the complexity of your opportunity.

Delivering on a new opportunity always requires something new even for the simplest opportunity. Take adding a menu item in an existing restaurant. What would that require to be successful? The recipe would have to be developed. Your requirements might be that the new recipe be tasty, look good, cooked within food cost allowances, and easy to prepare. It may need to be plated on current dishes or you may need a new dish for a stylized delivery. The name and description may need to fit in existing menu categories and so on.

New services too have new requirements. Resource may need new skills. Equipment necessary to deliver the services such as servers or laptops may need to be upgraded. Software tools may need to be purchased, tested, and even customized to ensure success. Standard contracts and templates may need to be agreed upon and developed. Branding may need to be considered and so on.

Products from software to toys must meet certain requirements as well. Some requirements may include that the product meets specifications, is user friendly, and so on. The detailed requirements of a successful product are unique to each product.

Making a checklist to be sure nothing is forgotten is a good best practice. Many times, the requirement checklist can be customized and used over and over again for similar opportunities. There are many templates available on the Internet on sites such as CapacitySquared.net

Designing. Your design phase may be simple or complicated. New products need specifications. Services may need parameters. One or more designs may be necessary before your design meets your requirements. You may need sketches, diagrams, images, and/or flowcharts to make your design clear. Engineering services, hardware products, and software offerings require design documents that meet industry standards.

Your service design sets the parameters for consistent high-quality delivery every time. It may include how customers are addressed, meetings are held, services are rendered, invoices are delivered, and so on.

Your product design may be as simple as how to create a new web page on a client's website. It may be as complex as how to build a bridge that withstands 70 mile per hour winds and torrential rainfall in heavy traffic. Whatever your opportunity, a well-executed design phase saves time and avoids issues when you are ready implement your opportunity.

Preparation. Many entrepreneurs only consider the design of their product and/or service in the design phase. However, the most successful businesses consider what it takes to offer the product or service as well. They know that if they get an order for 100,000 new widgets, they must be able to make them and ship them on time. Service companies benefit from taking a moment to consider what a successful delivery looks like as well. In both cases, you must set quality standards, determine what resources must be involved, and work out any issues that might delay successful delivery to a happy client or customer.

Consider the following:

- Business Structure
- Equipment
- Processes and Procedures

Business Structure

Make sure the right business structure is in place to support your success. Startups need to make sure that founding documents are in place. Ongoing businesses must look at the business to determine if the current structure works for the new opportunity.

Very young businesses with few people tend to operate without the structure and processes that supports good work and avoids chaos. All businesses experience growing pains. Understanding where those pains come from is the part of designing the infrastructure you need to support your opportunity. Often, when you think you have people problems, you really have process problems. In a paper published in the *Journal of Applied Behavior Analysis* by Donald Hantula, an associate professor specializing in organizational behavior research, revealed that optimizing a system as a whole led to better problem solving. What that means is most of the time when you think you have a bad employee or you just cannot find the right people, you actually have a disconnect in the processes that create your business structure. (Hantula 1995)

Designing your business structure takes time. However, if as you add people, you set organized expectations and add the processes to support success right away you get less resistance. It just becomes the way the business is done. No one likes change. There is a natural resistance to change even when it is clear to see the change is necessary and good. Ask more of your team when you are small so that they fall in line more quickly as you build your business.

Businesses with a solid business structure often incorporate the following:

- Plans that are clear with SMART goals that are specific, measurable, achievable, realistic, and time specific
- Policies and procedures that set the business standards for how you run your business that are easily understood and followed
- Workflows that are easy to follow that you use to help plan and manage well-ordered change when change is necessary
- Documented processes with written step-by-step repeatable procedures that help ensure the business runs consistently even during personnel changes
- Regular reports based on key performance indicators you use to measure whether or not goals are met
- Project plans for every project that clearly indicate the goals, the budget, the timeline, and the tasks assigned to specific employees with due dates
- Issues and Actions Item reports with assignments and deadlines that keep things from falling through the cracks

Equipment

Determine what equipment you need to build your product or create your service. You may need manufacturing equipment, new computers, or even workstations for new staff. Consider everything. Lease or purchase equipment necessary to build or test your prototype. Time the arrival of the equipment so that you have what you need just in time.

Do the same thing for any additional equipment necessary to deliver your product and/or service. Plan the timing of any equipment you need once you determine the prototype is successful. If you have a tight budget you may be considering leasing equipment, using a portion of a third-party warehouse to handle logistics (3PL), or a copacker for order fulfillment to reduce your upfront costs. Make those arrangements now so you know you can manufacture store, and ship your goods if you get a big order.

Documentation

You are about to take on something new. Understanding and communicating how that happens prevents costly mistakes and saves time. Many small business owners and leaders find that proper documentation is the secret of their success. Entrepreneurs who take the time to design their processes and procedures upfront are more likely to be successful. For many, this requires learning new skills.

Build Processes and Procedures That Work

Make your processes and procedures elegantly simple and easily repeatable so that anyone with the right skills and experience can be successful. It does not matter if you are making products or providing services, there is a process for everything you and your team do. Processes happen informally when no formal process exists.

Organic informal processes that are not documented and tested are more likely to be inconsistent, incomplete, and/or wrong. Document each process with workflows often called process maps and step-by-step instructions often called procedures. Test each one to be sure the processes you use are consistent, efficient, accurate, and complete. Doing so helps prevent mistakes and missteps that cost time and money.

When a business is well documented, each process map connects to one or more other process maps because no business action should stand alone. For example, you or your bookkeeper may need to pay bills documented in one process and accept payments documented in another. At the end of the month, you or your bookkeeper balances the books. These tasks are connected.

Choosing the Right Workflow Process Map

A workflow process map is basically an outline providing a picture of how things happen. The picture does not have to be complicated. Most business processes can be mapped by very simple process maps using a pen and paper or free or low-cost software. More complicated options exist to meet technical, regulatory, or complex requirements. Use the simplest map available that meets your needs.

Consider the process map options below:

- Simple (Low Level)
- Top Down
- Cross-Functional (Swim Lanes)
- Detailed
- Workflow With Pictures
- System Level

Simple Map

Use these maps to show day-to-day procedures that keep a business operating in a more or less linear fashion. Very few symbols are necessary (Figure 6.14). Anyone can do them. These maps have these characteristics in common:

- Arrows tend to flow in one direction.
- Processes are shown by a square process flow symbol.
- Decisions points are clearly indicated by diamonds.
- Connectors may be used to show how to move from one page to another.

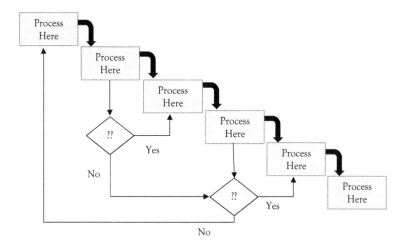

Figure 6.14 Process maps simple

Cross-Functional (Swim Lanes)

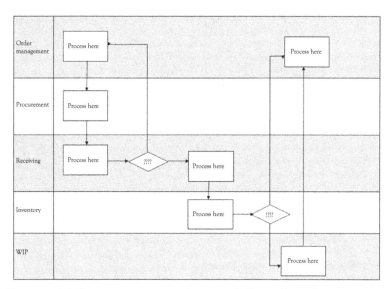

Figure 6.15 Process maps cross-functional (Swim Lanes)

Cross-functional maps (Figure 6.15) ae called Swim Lanes because of the horizontal lines used to separate functional areas that resemble the swim lanes in a pool. Use these maps to show processes that require more than one person to compete so that you can see how each process transitions from one functional area to another.

For example, sales may place an order, manufacturing builds the product, and shipping sends it to the customer. Many people representing more than one department may be involved. Swim Lane process maps make those transitions easier to see. Use these maps as you grow to help uncover process issues such as bottlenecks, repetitive processes, and missing processes.

Detailed

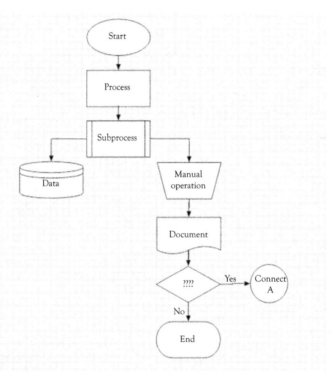

Figure 6.16 Process map detailed

Like simpler process maps, the detailed process map uses symbols (Figure 6.16). More symbols are used to demonstrate more complicated processes in greater detail. These maps use multiple symbols to visually separate processes, sub processes, documentation, data, and so on.

Legends are often used to help the reader better follow this map. Use these flows to document more intricate manufacturing, distribution, engineering, technical, and business processes. These maps are excellent for ISO 9000 manufacturing quality standards when you are seeking certifications.

Top-Down Map

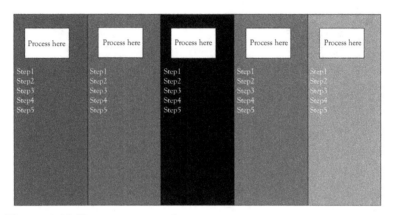

Figure 6.17 Process map top down

Top-down maps (Figure 6.17) use only one symbol to document a process and the steps that support it. Decision points are not included. The work is broken down in a picture that is easier to see. Processes best documented with this flow are quite simple and move only in one direction. The power of these flows is the ability to connect the corresponding steps to each process.

Use these flows to identify ways to create efficiencies in standard work processes by reviewing maps to make sure most efficient task order is followed or to look for duplicated efforts and unnecessary steps.

Many entrepreneurs use post it notes on a white board to build these maps so the processes can be moved around until everyone involved agrees the map is correct. Often, this map is used for brainstorming and design sessions because of the ease of making changes.

Workflow With Pictures

Workflow diagrams that forego standard map symbols for friendlier images may increase adoption (Figure 6.18). Use these maps to demonstrate processes for an audience who is unfamiliar with process flow techniques. These maps are frequently used in training sessions, investor sessions, and when working with an advisory board.

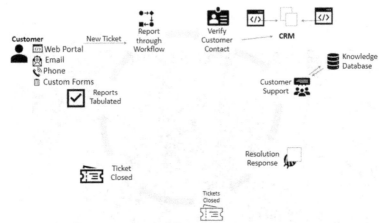

Figure 6.18 Process map workflow with pictures

System Level Process Map

System level maps (Figure 6.19) show the highest level of business processes in an organization. These maps are used to demonstrate business cycles such as cash flow, order to fulfillment, production, system development, and so on. Systems that are important to your opportunity can be reviewed using this type of map. Management teams use these maps to better understand the organization and interaction of a division or an entire company. Strategic partners may use these maps to separate partner responsibilities. Additionally, system maps are also often required to get ISO 9000 certification.

Power of Review

Documented processes often uncover issues. The power of the workflow process map is the ability to make changes on paper before mistakes happen. Review maps with anyone impacted to uncover bottlenecks, redundancies, or barriers to success. Consider efficiencies too especially in points of communication and handoffs. Oftentimes, just notifying a team member earlier eliminates surprises and reduces mistakes.

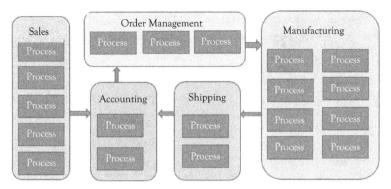

Figure 6.19 Process Map system level

Effective Process Checklist

Whenever you or your team creates processes use this checklist (Table 6.7) to review the final version.

Table 6.7 Effective Process Checklist

	Processes are accurate.
	Arrows are easy to follow.
	Wording is clear.
	Process is effective with no missing processes, or repeated processes.
	Process has no bottlenecks or barriers to success.
	Procedure is efficient. There are no changes that would make it better.

Procedures People Follow

While workflow process maps provide an outline of the tasks that must be accomplished, day-to-day work still must be done at a more detailed level. Procedures are just step-by-step instructions necessary to successfully complete a task. These instructions become your Standard Operating Procedures (SOPs). These instructions have a variety of uses. Use your SOPs to enforce accountability, set standards, and train.

Regardless of the use make sure your SOPs are easily understood. The way adults learn has evolved over time. There has been a lot of research over the last three decades on how adults learn. Out of that has come some very consistent ways to be successful in writing good instructions.

Good instructions have certain characteristics in common:

- Simple
- Purpose Driven
- Audience Focused
- Visual
- Brief
- Safe
- Numbered
- Clear
- Efficient and Effective

Simple

The main thing to remember is that good instructions are always simple. Anyone can make something complicated. It often takes a bit more effort to make instructions simple. Choose the simplest wording possible. As a rule, write at a seventh-grade level when writing to adults regardless of their education level. Even readers with graduate degrees appreciate simple easy-to-read instructions.

Purpose Driven

Tell people why they should care. Answer the four w's: who, what, when, and why in a short introductory paragraph. The how will come later in your step-by-step instructions.

Audience Focused

Every audience is a little different. You should always know your audience before you start. Write to the broader audience making sure that you write at a level the reader with the least experience and education can understand. Answer the following questions before you begin:

- What is the lowest level of education of my audience?
- What is the average education of my audience?
- How much experience does my average reader have?

- How little experience will my least experienced reader have?
- How familiar will my average reader be with this topic?
- How familiar will my least experienced reader be with this topic?
- How much skill will my average reader have regarding the task at hand?
- How much skill does the least experienced reader have with the task at hand?

Visual

Remember the old adage a picture is worth 1000 words. It is still true even in the 21st century. Whenever a picture adds clarity, use one. The only time you should skip illustrations is when the instructions are meant for an audience that is ALL expert. Experts consider pictures demeaning. The rest of your readers will be grateful for a picture (Figure 6.20). Videos are even better. This is why YouTube is so popular. Optional videos help beginners tremendously. However, expert readers often skip the visual instruction. Everyone wins.

Figure 6.20 Picture by Eileen Pan provided by Unslash

Brief

Simply said seven steps are best. Most every instruction you write can be broken down into five to nine steps. Memory works a lot like RAM on a computer. Just like a computer, readers access a small chuck of memory at a time. The rest of their knowledge is safely stored in the background in their brains. By breaking instructions into small groups of steps, you ask your reader to store the steps separated by headlines in memory the same way your reader will need to access them later, in small chunks.

For example, if a task has 27 steps that is hard for anyone to remember. Breaking the task into five to seven steps at a time improves the likelihood of success. If the task is to fix broken equipment, understanding the process task in small junks such as—Remove the cover, followed by Inspect the equipment, Identify and remove the broken piece, and Replace the cover—is easier to remember. If a reader knew everything but how to remove the broken piece, (s)he would only need to read that part of the procedure. Without headlines, the reader would have to read through all 27 steps wasting precious time.

Brief

Remember less is more. Like Twitter, sentences in instructions should be as short as possible. Click Save is better than Click the Save button to store the data. More words do not make the sentence clearer. In fact, more words may make the instruction more confusing. As a rule, make sentences no more than 23 words long. If you cannot say what needs to be said in 23 words, you have probably combined two steps into one. Separate the steps into two shorter sentences.

Safe

Make notes but give warnings. Put helpful information in Notes or Caution statements. If you think the reader needs extra information to be successful, be sure to add it. If there are no safety issues involved, add the additional information as a note. If, however, there is any danger of something harmful happening from losing important data to possible death, create a Caution or Warning message. Caution and Warnings should be the most prominent text on the page or screen.

Numbered

Steps should always be numbered. The purpose of the numbers is to indicate that order matters. Steps are linear. The instructions will not work if you do three first and five second. You must follow each direction in the order listed. On the other hand, if you have a list of criteria to be considered and none is more important than the other, then use a bullet list.

Clear

Avoid abbreviations and conjunctions such as BTW or can't that are not industry specific. Using abbreviations that only the inner circle understands invites errors. Use industry jargon only when it is appropriate for your audience. Write for experienced and inexperienced readers by spelling out words the first time used such as Small Business Administration (SBA). Use the abbreviation after the first introduction.

Avoid conjunctions as well. Many languages do not have conjunctions. Two words are never strung together like won't or can't. You should always assume you have a multicultural audience. Avoiding conjunctions avoids confusion.

Efficient and Effective

Once written and reviewed by those impacted, documented procedures often uncover issues that might not have been so easily found. Reviewers often see missing steps, bottlenecks, repeated steps, or barriers to success that can be corrected. They sometimes see efficiencies too. When everyone impacted has a chance to comment, it is not uncommon for teams to suggest changes that reduce the time it takes to compete tasks successfully.

Effective Procedure Checklist

Whenever you or your team writes procedures use this checklist (Table 6.8) to review the final version.

Prototype

Many people think of products when they think about prototypes. Traditionally, a prototype is the first product manufactured or produced ready to be tested to be sure your product works as well in reality as you

Table 6.8 *Effective Procedure Checklist*

	Procedures are accurate.
	Procedures can be completed in five to nine steps. Most are completed in seven.
	Steps that must be followed in order are numbered.
	Lists that do not require the reader to perform tasks in order use bullets.
	Sentences are short and to the point with no more than 23 words per sentence.
	Steps are easy to read and do not contain conjunctions such as can't or don't.
	Technical language and acronyms are not included except where needed for clarity.
	Punctuation is correct.
	Instructions are appropriate for the audience.
	Procedure is effective with no missing steps, bottlenecks, repeated steps, or barriers to success.
	Procedure is efficient. There are no changes that would make it better.

planned. However, prototyping is good for services as well. This is where you walk through delivering your service for a test subject to make sure your service meets the needs of your potential customers. If there are gaps in your delivery strategy, you want to know it before you try to deliver in front of a paying customer. Often, it takes more than one round to get it exactly right.

Go/No Go Decision

Yes. Congratulations your prototype suggests that your opportunity is solid. You are ready to move ahead.

No. Your prototype has proven that your opportunity is too risky to move forward.

Maybe. Your prototype has issues that can be fixed. Consider the time and expense of making changes to determine if you should move forward.

Develop

Whether you are developing software, producing a new product, or preparing to offer a new service the development phase prepares you for implementation. Everything that must be done to be ready for implementation must be finished in this phase. Development is more than the production of a product or service proven by a successful prototype. It is the process of preparing to fulfil contracts and orders for goods and/or services. Fully developing your opportunity looks different based on whether you are creating a product, delivering a new service, or both.

Technical, engineering, construction, and complex projects and products require their own development schedule with time estimates, task assignments, milestones, delivery dates, and status reports. You may need project planning software to successfully monitor this part of your development process. This is the time to put everything you need to be successful in place.

Determine what you need by answering these questions:

- Do I need a separate project plan to cover creating my product or service?
- What needs to be done to make space ready if needed?
- What must be done to set up any equipment identified during Design and Prep?
- What other purchases need to be made and when?
- Do I have quotes and proposals ready to answer Requests for Quotes and Requests for Proposals if necessary to sell to potential customers?
- Are procurement contracts in place to ensure the on-time delivery of any necessary materials?
- Will I need templates to produce consistent documentation and reports internally and externally for clients and customers?
- What branding and/or packaging does my product or service need?
- Does my website need to be created or updated to support my new opportunity?
- How will my clients/customers pay? What needs to be set up and tested?

- Does marketing and/or sales collateral need to be developed?
- What contracts do I need to have in place?
- What added resources do I need in place, if any?
- Do my resources need to be trained and if so, when to be ready to go?

Depending on your answers you may need a simple checklist or a detailed plan of action. Your answers may bring up even more questions for consideration. Taking time to do what you need to be prepared for success often makes the difference between success and failure.

Phase Four—Implementation

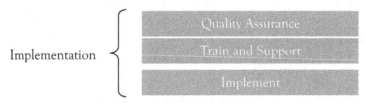

Figure 6.21 Opportunity Development Life Cycle phase four

Quality Assurance

Regardless of whether you are delivering goods and/or services you want to be sure your team delivers the very best quality possible. Define what quality looks like. Test to ensure you are delivering what your potential customer wants. While some products and technology may need very detailed and sometimes complex test plans, most goods and services can ensure quality more simply (Figure 6.21).

The best way to test is to predict scenarios that are likely to occur sometimes called use cases. Ask yourself what is likely to happen if someone orders your product or contracts for your service? Ask yourself what happens when things go predictably well and when things do not go perfectly. Project and quality management software application often include a feature to capture use cases. Spreadsheets like the example below (Table 6.9) may be used as well. A template is available at CapacitySquared.net.

Table 6.9 Testing Report

No.	Use Case	Tester Name	Test Date	Result	Notes

A use case may be as simple as my new menu items arrives hot to a customer up to 20 minutes away in the packaging selected. You may want to know that a customer is created with 10 seconds of walking in the door. On the other hand, your test may be complex such as data uploads into the right database tables without error taking no more than one minute for every 20,000 records. You may need test participants that are on and off site. You may test that your client can compete and sign contracts for your services online using the tools you selected. You may want to know that a client can pay for your new services by credit cards or ACH payments.

Consider all of the normal business procedures that contribute to the functions that support the success of your opportunity. Start with sales and end with payments. Consider the following to determine whether your new product or service meets your quality standards:

1. Develop your use case list.
2. Bring out your Requirements Checklist and use it to ensure that you are delivering what you planned and that your use case list covers each one.
3. Test to be sure specifications were followed if necessary.
4. Follow your workflows and process maps to test each is accurate and up-to-date.
5. Run through your procedures to be sure each of these are accurate and up-to-date and your team knows what is expected.
6. Check product packaging if applicable to make sure it meets your branding requirements and your customers' specifications.
7. Review online and paper marketing material to make sure it is ready and meets your branding standards.

Go/No Go Decision

Now is the time to consider if you are ready for implementation.

Yes. Congratulations you are almost at the end of your ODLC journey. Get your team(s) excited. If you have not already kicked off your marketing and sales campaigns, now is the time to start.

No. Sometimes it happens that you get this far before determining your opportunity will not work. It is good to know now before you move forward in a more public way.

Maybe. If you are running behind schedule or you found issues during quality assurance, you may want to address those issues before you move ahead. Other you may find that you must make modifications to your product and/or service before moving forward. You may even have to take a few steps back to ensure your opportunity is a success. Take the time to do it right.

Train and Support

Training may be necessary for your team members and/or your customers to be successful. Those who support your opportunity must be ready as well. Sometimes that requires internal training that must be developed and presented in training classes. Training may take days or weeks to prepare and deliver. Other team members need to improve their skills through external training when they are taking on new roles. This training must be budgeted, scheduled, and completed before implementation so that you are ready for success.

Distributors and customers may need to be trained as well in some circumstances. You must decide if that training happens in person or remotely.

Consider:

- Who needs to be trained?
- What training do they need?
- When do they need to be trained?

In order to answer these questions:

- Where does the training come from?
- How long will it take?
- How will it be delivered?
- How will new people be trained after implementation? Does the plan change for them?

Assign the appropriate resources and create a timeline to develop and deliver the training necessary for success. Reach out to professionals if training development is not in your business skill set. The investment in training pays dividends in the end.

Implement

An implementation plan is a checklist of everything that must be done to successfully to deliver your product and/or service after your first sale. Once the day has finally come, you want to be ready. Implementation plans may be simple or very complex depending on your product and/ or service.

After reviewing the processes and procedures necessary for the success of your implementation plan, answer these questions:

- Is the software and equipment planned for available and ready for use?
- Were the changes, if any, made to your workspace as required?
- Are the team members that must be in place to succeed trained and ready to go?
- What must you start doing?
- What must you stop doing?
- Which assignments have changed?

For simple implementations, just answering the questions may be enough to ensure your team is ready to go. Complex implementations require a plan. If once you answer these questions, you realize a plan is required, make one now. Include the task, the resource assigned, the estimated start date, and end date and a status. The key to staying on track is to be sure the task is clear, there is a resource assigned, and a deadline to avoid miscommunications. If starting one task is contingent on another being finished note that as well. Implementation plans (Table 6.10) can be created using most project management software application or any spreadsheet as shown.

Table 6.10 Implementation Plan

Task No.	Contingent Task No.	Task	Assigned	Start Date	End Date	Status	Notes

Make sure assigned resources report their status and raise any issues that might prevent success. Issues may be tracked on your plan or as part of a separate Issues Report.

Go/No Go Decision

Yes. You are ready to go and headed for success. Celebrate and move forward.

No. Despite your high hopes, you are not ready to implement because something has gone wrong you cannot fix.

Maybe. Consider what you can do to save your investment. Perhaps changes to your opportunity or more time to prepare will make your opportunity a success. Plan to get back on track if possible.

Phase Five—Review

Review $\left\{\rule{0pt}{12pt}\right.$

Figure 6.22 Opportunity Development Life Cycle phase five

Once you complete the ODLC cycle take a step back and consider all you learned (Figure 6.22). Reflect upon what you would do if you had it to do all over again. Bring your team together to document your lessons learned.

Consider these questions:

- What went right?
- What went wrong?
- How can we improve next time?
- What processes and procedures need to be updated based on the answers to the first three questions?

Assign team members to update the processes and procedures you identified in a specified time period. Follow up to make sure the work gets done as expected.

CHAPTER 7

Where

The best way to predict your future is to create it

—Peter Drucker

Location, Location, Location

Your future could be literally anywhere in the 21st century. The Covid-19 pandemic pushed an already growing virtual office trend into a work from home norm. For any entrepreneur utilizing a remote work team, managing the work environment is essential to success. Clearly, there are exceptions to remote teams. If your company manufactures and/or distributes products, the team must work together. Brick and mortar stores from retail to restaurants require onsite teams as well. Trade service companies may or may not have sites where technicians come to get work vans and/or equipment. Some companies utilize remote teams to serve their customers' needs anywhere in the country and for global companies, anywhere in the world.

When Location Matters

Obviously, if your team comes together for any part of the work week or day, then where you choose to set up shop matters. Your site must be convenient to your resources and your customers regardless of whether they come to you, or you go to them. This seems obvious, however often putting some thought into where helps ensure your success.

Whether you are picking a site, changing sites, or validating that your current site still works ask yourself these questions:

- What is most important about my business location?
- How far will customers come if they need to come to my site?

- How far will resources come if they need to drive to my site all or part of the week?
- Can my business thrive with remote resources?

Your team wants to be safe. Avoid high crime areas. If public transportation is important to your team members, consider that as well. Workers may avoid businesses that require them to walk long distances regardless of weather conditions and may not consider walking in high crime areas at all.

People will drive only so far to shop and to work. When jobs are readily available, workers who love where they work still switch jobs to reduce or eliminate commute time. Customer loyalty is impacted by ease of access as well. A customer really must love what you do to drive past four other places that do the same thing to get to you.

Follow the steps below to validate your current site or select a new one:

Step One—Prepare for Your Review

1. Review industry data to find out how far your customers are likely to travel to get to you.
2. Reread the information from your buyer profile to determine the likelihood that your buyer will be loyal specifically to you.
3. Use data about your area from Census.gov to determine where your likely buyers work and live.
4. Purchase or print a map of the area.
5. Purchase or gather multiple multicolored push pins.

Step Two—Review Your Location(s) Option(s)

1. Put the map on cardboard so that you can stick pins in it.
2. Use red push pins to indicate your site options and insert the pins.
3. Use additional push pins to locate your competitors:
   - Blue within a 1 mile radius
   - Green 2 to 5 mile radius
   - Yellow 6 to 10 mile radius

4. Use white push pins to indicate areas where your customers live and work and circle your service areas.
5. Use clear push pins to show where your resources who commute to your location tend to live.
6. Calculate and write down the total of site-specific costs that are important to you depending on owning or renting next to your site option(s) on the map.
7. Review your map to make a site decision.

Thriving From Anywhere

If getting together in person is passé for your team, make your remote work environment work as your primary focus. Companies that allow work from home, use remotely stationed work teams, and/or have field technicians often find it takes more effort to build a positive accountable team-oriented culture.

All groups who work together for a common objective or goal create a culture. The culture for virtual work is the same as the culture for onsite work. Done well, the ability to spread out can actually help build value and add capacity to your organization.

Here are useful strategies for any environment where team members work remotely:

- Enable Chatting
- Provide Easy Collaboration
- Schedule Efficient Meetings
- Require Status Reporting

Enable Chatting

Make conversations easy. When your team members work in offices, they learn by overhearing conversations and chatting in the breakroom. Field technicians and remote workers miss that. A good group chat emulates that shared experience of conversation. Chat applications give your remote team members a way to ask a question or get assistance quickly as well.

Clearly, you want your team to be responsible and use chat mostly for business purposes. Be sure, most of the conversations are at least peripherally related to work because you want your teams to be productive. However, permitting your team members to do the same kind of casual check ins they would do with each other at work builds repour. Asking if someone feels better after an illness or if they enjoyed the game on TV last night should be accepted. Only step in if the chats get too busy with personal threads. Use your team leaders to redirect the focus. Checking on your teams is important too. Build comradery by asking the team "How are you?" in chat once a week.

Easy Collaboration

It is important to remember that even when working together in one office space, not every moment is a collaborative moment. Most of the time your team needs space to focus and get their work done. Nurture collaboration with brainstorming sessions and brown bag lunches. Sessions and lunches do not have to be remote, but they can be. Make these gatherings less formal than meetings and throw in a bit of fun occasionally.

Encourage socializing. Plan team events more often to encourage friendships among coworkers with happy hours or team dinners. Ask your team members what they would like to do and center fun around their interests. If team members are too remote for such get togethers consider bringing the team together once or twice a year for a few days of team building.

When teams do need to collaborate closely or when group deadlines require quick responses, create a remote shared space. Start a conference or video call at the beginning of the day and leave it going whether anyone is using it or not. Require all team members involved to be logged in and muted unless they are in another meeting. This emulates the ability to walk up to a team member and ask a question, get status, or ask for help. Team members can quickly ask for a side meeting with one or more of the team if needed. Group calls also prevent urgent issues from being stuck in e-mail, missed in text, or ignored in chats avoiding common remote work delays.

Reinforced Deadlines

Make sure promises made are promises kept. This is the best way to know your remote team members are as productive as they would be working in an office with you. Deadlines for deliverables, for resolving issues and or taking promised action should be regularly enforced. If attendees agree to do something, they should report back on the status of the task until it is complete.

Require Status Reports

Weekly status reports (Figure 7.1) are one of those things some entrepreneurs consider busy work. However, in a remote culture that reinforces accountability, it is essential that you and your team leaders have a way to track the work being done. Some people have trouble organizing themselves when they are in a less formal environment. Being required to report work planned, in process, and work completed helps disorganized team members get organized. Field technician status reports help keep field workers on target to meet weekly goas as well.

These reports should take between 10 and 30 minutes to complete. The best way to know if your team is accomplishing what they set out to do is to get each team member to tell you in writing. It can be as simple as:

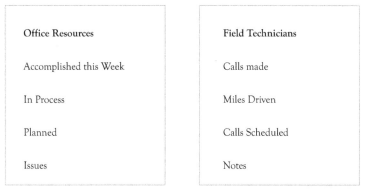

Office Resources	Field Technicians
Accomplished this Week	Calls made
In Process	Miles Driven
Planned	Calls Scheduled
Issues	Notes

Figure 7.1 Status Report Templates

Work Planned should move to In Process and then Accomplished. If work is not moving from Planned to Accomplished, there is an issue to resolve. Issues should go from Open to Resolved. This helps:

- Your resource plan and organize their work.
- Your resource and your team leaders know where people are stuck or have missed something.
- You recognize if resources are becoming overloaded or bottlenecked.
- You feel comfortable that work is being accomplished.

Leaders who receive reports should regularly respond with questions or praise so that your resources know their reports matter.

CHAPTER 8

Change

You cannot become what you want to be by remaining what you are.
—Mae Depree

Managing Change Without Chaos

Change happens even in the most stable organization. Change happens even after you spent time and money getting everything to work just right. Change happens because the world around us changes so rapidly. A large part of what thriving businesses do better than those that are less successful is plan for, control, and manage change. According to Deloitte Global CEO Punit Renjen, resilient businesses have five traits that allow them to thrive even under extreme conditions. These traits include being "prepared, adaptable, collaborative, trustworthy, and responsible." Change broken down into an organized step-by-step process using best practices that embody Renjen's five traits of resilience becomes manageable. (Renjen 2021)

Status quo is comfortable even when not efficient or effective. Change, no matter how beneficial, always causes some pushback and discomfort. Often, even minor changes cause anxiety. It does not have to be that way. Entrepreneurs and business leaders who follow best practices build change resilience organizations that embrace constant process improvement do better than those who do not.

The 2021 Deloitte Global resilience report found that: "Perhaps most importantly, the data suggests that speed matters. Organizations that made early investments in change-resilient strategies during the Covid-19 crisis— or, even better, had already made strategic, workforce, and technology investments in capabilities that enhance resilience—outperformed their competition." (Renjen 2021) At the beginning of the pandemic according to the SBA Office of Small Business Advocacy, there were approximately thirty million small businesses in the United States. After only 12 months, 843,229 appeared to have gone away. (SBA 2021) Those who managed change survived.

Entrepreneurs that define change initiatives in ways that their team members understand and support become empowered to succeed repeatedly. When you face the initial discomfort head on, you build change-resilient teams. This is important to success because change is necessary for growth. The faster you grow, the more change your team members' experience. Anything that makes change easier reduces risk.

There are big changes such as selling the business, growing through acquisition, merging, bringing in a new partner, or rapidly pivoting in crisis which only happen rarely. Small changes happen all the time. New leaders are brought in and new team members are hired. New opportunities require shifting and reorganizing. Growth requires more formal procedures to ensure consistency across your organization. Owners and leaders delegate to free up time for other business priorities.

How do you know that change is necessary? Your processes stop working smoothly. You notice:

- Team members get surprised and you find they are not ready when handed work.
- Resources argue and point fingers when something goes wrong.
- Someone has to step up as a superhero to save the day to deliver usually by many hours of overtime, sourcing materials at the last minute, or making some other heroic effort.
- One or more of your team members spends a good deal of time handling small emergencies often referred to as fighting fires.

While it can be tempting to blame your resources, these are all indications that one or more of your processes are broken. W. Edwards Deming who taught at New York and Columbia Universities while consulting with some of the biggest manufacturing companies of his time is known as the father of process improvement. He was known to say, "Put a good person in a bad system and the bad system wins, no contest." He would also frequently say, "Eighty-five percent of the reasons for failure are deficiencies in the systems and process rather than the employee. The role of management is to change the process rather than badgering individuals to do better." (Deming, Orsini, and Cahill 2012)

Change happens in a myriad of ways. To manage change, avoid implementing too many changes at one time. Many think that change can happen overnight not realizing that lasting successful change is actually a long-term process. Large organizations manage the process of change with a change initiative budget that includes hiring skilled professionals. Small businesses do not often have the luxury of that support as they face the same challenges. For this reason, changing slowly over time makes sense.

Regardless of your business size, follow change management best practices to build change resilient teams. Following the steps of solid change management best practices for every little change makes making big changes easier for everyone. Many times, leaders get in the way of resiliency trying to save money and time by skipping essential change management steps.

They ignore best practices and instead begin without a clear starting point or without identifying and involving the right people. Skipping those essential first steps is like building a house without a sound foundation. It is impossible to know what lies ahead. Cracks soon appear.

Change may not look big on the surface as in the case of a small plane engine manufacturer who acquired a midsize boat engine plant. It appeared the new organization would merge seamlessly into the current company infrastructure. However, they discovered far too late each had very different accounting, pricing, and inventory practices. Current systems were not scalable or flexible enough to handle all the new requirements that kept popping up during the merger integration. The integration project had to start over at the beginning. Missing steps cost money and time.

Even something as small as partnering two team members to take on a big project who have always worked individually requires some thought and preparation. Much like the engine company, the new partners may have different ways of approaching the same work. Taking a moment to go through the steps of change management reduces the change of friction and increases the chances of success.

Change-resilient businesses follow a process for every change because it works. Small changes often happen in a day. Large changes that impact an entire organization may take years. Large or small, the characteristics of a thorough change strategy are the same:

- Proper Review
- Transparent Goals
- Obtainable Metrics
- Resistance Management
- Identified Stakeholders
- Engaged Subject Matter Experts
- Well Developed Milestones
- Clear Communication
- Suitable Documentation, Training, and Support
- Reinforcement Follow-Up

Review Processes and Procedures

Asking for change without considering what happens to everyone impacted is like taking a trip without knowing where to start. Taking time to understand exactly what happens today provides a starting point that reduces the chance of making a change that causes more problems than it solves.

Review by:

1. Host a meeting including everyone impacted by the problem.
2. Review your current process workflow and associated procedures. Note: If your current process workflow and associated procedures are not documented, take the time to document them now.
3. Consider what must change to make the process(es) work better.
4. Walk through the solution taking time to consider how your changes could impact others or cause new problems.
5. Keep working together until you come to an agreement that works for everyone.
6. Update the processes and procedures.

Always consider that a change may make one team member's work easier but make another team member's work much more difficult and time-consuming. Following changes through the entire workflow system pinpoints possible issues.

Transparent Goals

Change does not happen in a vacuum. There is always some need. Develop clear goals that include the benefits and share them. All successful change begins with the end in mind. When your resources understand what success looks like and why success is important, they tend to get on board much faster. According to John Humphreys assistant professor of management at Eastern New Mexico University, ". . . to remain competitive today, firms need the valuable expertise and enthusiastic commitment of employees at every level. If handled properly, effective goal setting will enable the organization to benefit from both." (Humphreys 2003) Transparent goals create a much straighter path to success EVEN when those goals are not popular with everyone impacted.

Goals range from simple to very complex. However, the process of managing change remains the same. It does not matter how different the goals may be. For example, if you reduce the workload of an overworked team member by shifting responsibilities, automate work with new software, develop and market a new product or service, or merge with another company best practices required to implement the change remain the same. It is clear to see that when you work change management best practices into your culture as a standard of how to handle change, your company becomes more agile and resilient.

Obtainable Metrics

Create obtainable KPIs. Research shows that even in simple delegation providing a clear understanding of how soon the team member should become proficient and what that looks like increases the likelihood of better outcomes. When your team members understand what is expected they know to be successful.

KPIs become goals. Researchers Edwin Locke and Gary Latham proposed, "There is strong reason to conclude that goal setting works at the group and organizational (or unit) level as well as at the individual level." Their research showed team members were more successful when they were given feedback on their progress. KPIs provide the opportunity to provide that feedback and the encouragement necessary to create lasting change. (Locke, Latham 2013)

Resistance Management

Start by recognizing that resistance is just part of change. Resistance is natural. No one likes change. How you manage resistance is what matters. When you work to engage your team members instead of expecting them to fall in line without any understanding your chances of success grow. Engagement reduces the turbulence of disruption. Inspire your teams with a vision of how making the change required benefits them. Answer the question, "What is in it for me?"

Identify Stakeholders

Identify and align stakeholders which may be inside or outside your business. Understanding when changes impact your customers, your suppliers, and any other outsiders critical to your business helps you consider all those affected. Avoid surprises. Engage stakeholders as your team of advocates by telling them what is in it for them as well. Encourage your stakeholders to think about their own roles, their team roles, the business, and even your culture. Let stakeholders offer insights that help ensure success.

Engage Subject Matter Experts

A Subject Matter Expert (SME) is anyone with knowledge. SMEs might know what happens today or what must happen for your change to be successful. SMEs may understand a function, lead a department, or be experts. Engage your SMEs in identifying and creating the processes necessary for success. Use feedback to gain a better understanding, avoid risks, and overcome hurdles.

Well-Developed Milestones

Plan well using clearly defined milestones like all other plans that create a path of obtainable goals. Even the smallest change works better when it goes according to a plan. Simple plans might be agreed to in an e-mail. More complicated plans may require more in-depth documentation using spreadsheets or project management tools. There is at a minimum an agreement, a start, an implementation, and success. Celebrate milestone achievements. Maintaining the momentum necessary for success helps keep your team members feeling appreciated which builds change resiliency.

Clear Communication

Clear communication helps eliminate disruptive rumors while preparing and inspiring your team. Use a communication strategy whether you are putting out an e-mail to announce a promotion or following a formal communication plan to keep your stakeholders engaged in big change. Use your communication strategy to constantly align any change with your company's mission, vision, values, and goals.

Develop a strategy that fits within your company culture. Unread or unheard information is not useful and so your strategy must take into account how your stakeholders share information. Use the tools that are most effective for your teams in your communications. Town halls, e-mails, newsletters, intranet sites, regular meetings, video conferencing, and even tweets work when used properly.

Suitable Documentation, Training, and Support

Provide proper documentation, training, and support. Fear of the unknown causes resistance. Your team members want to be successful. As change happens, team members deserve the support necessary for success.

Develop and follow up on documentation, training goals, and objectives that show your team the benefits of success. When your employees understand how they can do their jobs better, faster, and easier than before they become advocates for the change. A well-written procedure, a useful checklist, and just enough training provides your team with the opportunity to succeed.

Reinforcement Through Follow-Up

Humans are creatures of habit. New habits take time to develop. Often, people slip back into the old way without even realizing what happened. Team members most resistant to change may even be waiting to revert when no one is looking.

Reinforce change by regularly following up on KPIs for 30 to 90 days provides accountability that incentivizes compliance until new habits form. After new habits form, going back begins to be considered an unwelcome change. At that point, the process is complete. Routine follow-up is the most important characteristic of a good change strategy important to making sure change lasts.

Managing Your Changing Team

Growth causes change. The challenge becomes how to create, build, add resources, and acquire skills quickly enough to make the growth profitable but not so fast as to create chaos. Sometimes managing efficiently means that better practices and automation cause teams to change. Your resources may need to move to new positions, new team members may be required, and others may choose to leave without being replaced.

Characteristics of good team management include:

- Writing Good Job Descriptions
- Hiring Well
- Delegating Your Way to Success
- Motivating Your Team
- Avoiding Burnout
- Understanding the People You Picked
- Embracing Turnover

Writing Good Job Descriptions

Positive change comes with good boundaries. Preparing a job description that defines expectations up front avoids having acquaintances, friends, and family members just create the job they want by only doing those things they enjoy. If you have resources in undefined positions then now is the time to become clearer.

Job descriptions do not need to be more than one or two paragraphs. Examples are on every job posting board. Some job posting boards provide you with templates and exercises to help you write better job descriptions for free. Once you have an accurate job description, it becomes easier to look on job boards to see what other similarly sized organizations are paying. Pay attention to the lowest and the highest offers to predict a more accurate pay range. Remember everyone wants their compensation to increase over time and so understanding where to start when you make job offers or give promotions allows room in your budget for increases.

Hiring Well

As you grow you may need and want more resources. Well-planned hiring builds strong teams. Hiring with a plan allows you to consider your real needs instead of just hiring another pair of hands. After all hiring people and filling jobs are two different things. Hiring slowly and carefully reduces your risks.

Be flexible to find just the resources you need at just the time you need them. Lin O'Neill, CEO of O'Neill Enterprises and Lead Faculty and Facilitator for 10,000 Small Businesses, is fond of saying, "Hire slow and fire fast." She encourages small business owners to use a contract to hire approach to be sure the resource is a good fit before making a commitment. (O'Neill 2021) Using a contract to hire approach allows you to contract with someone for 30 to 90 days before offering full-time employment. Both you and your candidate have the opportunity to determine if the job is both a good fit and a good match before committing.

Use independent contractors and gig workers when your need is temporary. These contractors are self-employed and thus provide their own benefits and pay their own taxes. Independent contractors and gig workers fill in your gaps for projects, large contracts, and seasonal needs. Avoid using contractors to keep from paying employee taxes or to give benefits to some of your team and not others because that is illegal.

Make sure your contractors meet the required Internal Revenue Service (IRS) guidelines of contractors. Per the IRS, "The general rule is that an individual is an independent contractor if the payer has the right to control or direct only the result of the work and not what will be done and how it will be done." (IRS 2021)

Sometimes however, what you need is a skilled and experienced resource for just 10 to 30 hours a week. It is not unusual for a growing business to need part-time professionals. Often, a more experienced part-time resource will move your company toward your goal without breaking your budget. Look for these resources among graduate students with real world experience, recently retired workers, and parents with young children. Consider using part-time professional focused job boards such as the one at CapacitySquared.net.

Hiring Resources

Your resources may include individual contributors, supervisors, managers, and part-time professionals. Often, it is tempting to hire people you know without going through a professional hiring process. However, even if you are sure you know who you want, taking your candidate through the hiring process is important. The hiring process confirms you made the right decision. Go through every step including and maybe most importantly checking references and the candidate's background.

Follow these steps:

1. Identify the need
2. Review or write a job description
3. Recruit candidates
4. Interview candidates
5. Check references and the candidate's background
6. Make an offer in writing even if just by e-mail
   Note: Do not use text for a written offer. You want to keep a historical record of the offer and texts tend to go away after time.
7. Onboard your new resource following your state and federal guidelines

Hiring Fractional Leaders and Experts

Fractional leaders are part-time C-suite and senior leadership professionals who provide strategic leadership services to businesses as a contractor not an employee as discussed before. Experts are those resources who know how to do work you do not. Both often have wisdom and experience outside of the skills and training of anyone else on your team.

What to Avoid

Properly vet candidates. There are all kinds of people claiming to be experts. Avoid those who are not such as:

- Fake experts
- Impersonators
- Fraction candidates with no fractional experience

Fake Exerts

Fake experts are those people who target inexperienced clients by using buzzwords from books they once read. These resources do not really have the wisdom and experience necessary to lead a growing company into the future. Fake experts have not really held the position for which they are asking to be hired. They speak with confidence because they read books.

Candidates who lack experience struggle to answer practical questions about how to operate because these candidates know theory and not practice. Be sure to ask very practical questions and expect the candidate to detail one or more real-life scenarios when answering.

Impersonators

Impersonators may have actually worked in the field, but they exaggerate their actual work experience. One exaggeration may be that they reached a higher role in their previous work experience than is actually true. Another exaggeration may be that they do not have the number of years of experience they actually claim. Many impersonators may hold certifications from groups that do little if any vetting. These groups teach a weeklong class and then provide expensive certificates after the payment clears. Carefully check out any certification programs your expert relies upon for credibility.

No Fractional Experience

Just having had years of experience in a larger company, even in a leadership role is not enough to make someone a good fractional leader. A good fractional leader often has consulting experience. Consultants learn to lead people who do not actually work in a subordinate role to them.

These leaders need to develop and implement key business strategies while helping your team build best practice procedures oftentimes without any direct authority. For some leaders, this is a difficult transition. Fractional leaders must have the wisdom and experience to guide others to do what is necessary even when they are not around to monitor progress.

Fractional leaders are the harbinger of change. A fractional leader must convince your team to make the changes required for your success. For this reason, the skills required of consultants tend to work better than the skills required of someone who has worked in a larger business for many years. The best fit may be someone who has done both.

What to Look for in Experts

Hiring experts who know more than you should not be intimidating. You are paying your experts to be the one who knows. You must ask them to prove that is true.

Look for:

- Intelligent Questions
- Confidence
- Practical Plans
- Decision Points
- Clear Expectations
- Examples of Success

Intelligent Questions

Experts have a responsibility to make sure that they only accept assignments where they believe they can be useful. During an interview, a candidate should not just be trying to convince you to sign a commitment contract. An experienced expert asks questions about your business, your experience, and most importantly your team. Your answers determine whether there is a good potential match between your business and the expert's experience. A good leader never accepts assignments that are not a good match.

Confidence

Watch experts for an air of wisdom and experience behind their words. Watch for sincerity when you ask hard questions. You want a leader who is never afraid to tell you hard truths. Someone who is timid or unsure will not gain the confidence of your team. Give each candidate a moment to consider answers to hard questions. Experienced experts are not afraid to take the time to answer questions correctly.

Practical Plans

Experts talk in terms of high-level practical plans that may include the pros and cons of more than one pathway forward. This may be the most crucial factor in making your selection. Experienced experts know how to do the job. Candidates should outline at a high level the steps that are necessary for success. They are not worried that if they give you the details about what needs to be done, you may decide to do it yourself. These experts know if you had the desire, experience, and time to do what you need, you would not be looking for someone else to take those steps for you. They believe that if by hearing the plan, you now think you can do the work yourself, you should.

Decision Points

Experts must display the confidence required to tell you what kinds of decisions you need to make to be successful. A good candidate clearly understands that you as a business owner are the one who is taking all the risk. A good match explains all the ramifications of a choice without needing to convince you to take one path or another.

Clear Expectations

Good candidates understand the results that can be achieved specific to the resources that are available. A good candidate offers a clear picture of expectations that should seem realistic to you. After gaining an understanding of your goals, an experienced candidate must offer a reasonable determination of the amount of time it would take to be successful as well. If the timeline is clearly too short or too long, that indicates a lack of experience.

Examples of Successes

Candidates with years of experience have success stories. The ability to tell a short and concise success story is one of the ways these experts gain the confidence of teams who must follow their direction. If a potential candidate does not offer any success stories during your interview there is cause for concern. Like any other candidate, your candidate must offer good references. Your candidate must support be both a fit and match. Do not skip the steps for hiring well.

Delegating Your Way to Success

Part of constant process improvement and managing change as you grow is knowing when and how to delegate. Delegate well to build a business that is agile, flexible, and resilient. It is clear to see how when you delegate well the company is more efficient and effective. Resources are more likely to do the right work at the right time.

Having your resources do the work they are best suited for saves your business money. Freeing up time for your leadership resources to do the work for which they are best suited may even improve your bottom line as well. Using people who are overpriced to do tasks at a premium gets expensive fast.

For example, no one would walk into a print shop and say I know you charge five cents a copy, but I want to pay you seventy five cents instead. However, many entrepreneurs walk by a team lead whom they pay $50 an hour making copies instead of an admin whom they pay $15 without a thought.

Not everyone has a team big enough to delegate. However, once you do it makes sense to create a frugal culture where employees collaborate to assign and do work in the most budget friendly way. You might even consider bringing on a part-time staffer or gig worker to free up team members who could be producing more income for you.

For example, there was a gentleman who owned a growing engineering firm. He took time away from billable hours to do all the purchasing himself. He hated procurement tasks and often the firm would run out of necessary items before he reordered slowing work. He thought he was showing that he was a team player.

Once he let go of the job and gave it to someone who did not do billable work, his team got supplies and he made more money. His team was happier too. They were able to bill more hours with less frustration. It turned out that they did not want him to be an equal member of the team so much as they wanted the supplies they needed to do their jobs.

What to Delegate

How do you know what to delegate? Ask yourself these three questions:

Is the Task Being Done in a Timely Manner Today?

Delegate the duties that you or your team most procrastinate about now. If you find that those mundane tasks that must be done keep getting put off then these are duties to delegate. As soon as possible, assign those tasks to someone more appropriate.

Is the Best Person Assigned to Do This Task?

Delegate tasks to resources who are better equipped to do them. If you are not an accountant or bookkeeper and you hate to do your finances, there is certainly someone better at it who loves numbers. In fact, you may have someone on your team who will do it in less time than it takes you currently.

Is This the Best Use of Time?

Time is a finite resource. Make sure your resources use time wisely. Never suggest a team member work overtime when another with the right skills does not have enough work. Conversely consider adding resources even temporarily at peak moments to ensure quality on-time delivery. Take time to weigh the long-term cost of missing a deadline or doing shoddy work against the short-term cost of getting more help.

How to Delegate

Once you are clear about what you want to delegate, consider how. The most common cause of delegation failure is a bad delegation process. Small business owners and leaders often give up on delegating thinking it is easier to do the work themselves. They get frustrated when sometimes the task is not done perfectly right away. They forget it may have taken them sometime to do the task as well. If you have been known to say that then you might be right once or twice. However, the cost of continuing to do work better done by someone else soon outweighs the temporary discomfort of delegation.

Delegating well begins with proper preparation and ends with reinforcement through follow-up. Make sure the process you want to delegate is documented. When your team members know what is expected of them and what it takes to be successful, they are more likely to meet your expectations.

Each time you or your team members prepare to delegate, ask this brief list of questions. When you know all of the answers, you are ready to begin:

1. What process would you like to transfer?
2. How is it done today?
3. Who is impacted and how are they impacted?
4. When will you delegate the process?

5. Who would you delegate the process to? (name or new employee)
6. How will you communicate the change?
7. How will you prepare your employee for success?
8. How long will it take before the employee can handle the job alone?
9. How will you know the process has been transferred successfully?

Once you are clear, meet with your employee or contractor. Using a script to make sure you do not miss anything often helps (Figure 8.1). It may feel awkward at first, but soon it will be a natural habit.

[Name Here] I have a task I would like you to take on for me. The task is [Task Name]. I want you to follow the process we have documented at [handbook / work procedure document / checklist]. [I/Your manager/supervisor] will provide you with all of the assistance you need to be successful by:

[list of steps here]

I expect you will be able to handle the task by [Date]. I will know you are ready to handle the task yourself by

[list of KPIs here]

Figure 8.1 Delegation template

For example, Joe, I have a task I would like you to take on for me. The task is posting to our social media accounts once per day. I want you to follow the process we have documented in our media standard operating procedures making sure to utilize the social media calendar and checklist. I will provide you with all of the assistance you need to be successful:

- First, we will walk through the process together.
- Next, I will watch you.
- After that, I will be available for questions for the next week.

I expect you will be able to handle the task by the end of a week. I will know you are ready to handle the task yourself when you have no questions and there have been no errors for 30 days.

Maintaining Employee Motivation

Money and titles are not the only motivation for people. Small businesses attract people who enjoy the benefits of working for smaller companies. Money matters, this is true. The Deloitte Global Millennial Survey 2020 showed that 69 percent of millennials admitted that they are motivated by the possibility of making more money as they move forward in their careers (Figure 8.2). What was surprising though was the same study showed that 71 percent were motivated by diversity and inclusion in their work environment. Another 69 percent reported impact to be important. It is clear to see that job loyalty rises as you address employee needs. Job satisfaction depends on many factors within your control. (Deloitte Inc 2020)

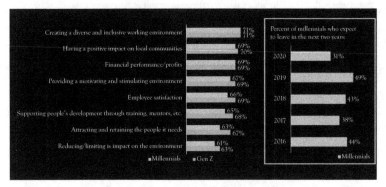

Figure 8.2 Deloitte Global Millennial Survey 2020

Understanding what matters most to your team gives you the opportunity to increase your team members' engagement. Doing so can be a win/win situation. Often, your efforts to engage your team work to your benefit as well. Consider, for example, embracing diversity in your hiring. According to the McKinsey and Company 2020 study, Diversity Wins, "In the case of ethnic and cultural diversity, our business-case findings are equally compelling: in 2019, top-quartile companies outperformed those in the fourth one by 36 percent in profitability, slightly up from 33 percent in 2017 and 35 percent in 2014."

Providing Training

When your team knows more and gets better at doing their work you benefit. Encourage even require your team members to continue to learn and grow throughout their career. Consider requiring a certain number of hours of training each year for yourself and your team members. According to the 2020 Training Industry Report, independent researchers found that small businesses on average provided 41.7 hours of training per employee while larger companies averaged 55.4. The reason most given for lack of training was cost. (Training Magazine 2020)

Training does not have to be a big-ticket budget item. There are many free and low-cost options available through colleges, nonprofits, and online courses. Constantly improve by building a better, faster, highly skilled team from within through continuous education.

Avoiding Burnout

Burnout causes a high performer to gradually slip, develop a bad attitude, or become lethargic. "The most important burnout symptom is the feeling of total exhaustion—to the extent that it cannot be remedied by normal recovery phases of an evening, a weekend, or even a vacation," per Christian Dormann PhD chair of business education and management at the Johannes Gutenberg-University. Most concerning was that after reviewing 48 studies on burn out from 1986 through 2019, Dormann discovered that the average age when people begin to experience burn out has gone down from 42 to 32. (Dormann and Gutenberg 2020)

When employees have been around for a very long time, they tend to become stuck. At some point, they cannot move forward. Improve the work of low performers who used to do well by asking them what they want. Consider moving low performers into other positions that better matches their interests now. Introduce new challenges into their daily routine. Recovering a burned out team member is far less expensive than hiring and training a new person.

You may well find they have reached the top of their pay range and there is no promotion available. They need other motivations to stay happy in their jobs. A study reported by *The Journal of Labor and Economics* showed: "Lower happiness is systematically associated with lower productivity." Reach out to understand what other factors are important to keep your team members engaged and if you cannot consider helping your once valuable team member find their dream job, somewhere else. (Oswald, Proto, and Sgroi 2015)

As a business grows, jobs get more defined. Individuals who wore many hats may now wear only one. Reporting requirements may increase as well taking away some of that prized autonomy. A once happy resource can become frustrated. When that happens, you do better to set your unhappy employee free to be happy. The job is no longer a match even if it still a fit.

Understanding the People You Picked

You built your team and you want the theory of how your team would work together to be as good at the reality. To make that happen, it pays to nurture your team members. It pays to understand them and make sure you are getting the full benefit of their skills and talents.

Personality Testing to Increase Understanding

People think differently. When you build teams with different perspectives, you build in resilience. You are less likely to be surprised. Creating teams with different leadership styles and communication styles creates cognitive diversity. Juliet Bourke, a consulting partner at Deloitte, defined cognitive diversity, "By cognitive diversity, we are referring to educational and functional diversity, as well as diversity in the mental frameworks that people use to solve problems. A complex problem typically requires input from six different mental frameworks or 'approaches' . . . hence; the need for complementary team members." (Bourke 2018)

However, having team members who think and lead differently creates the possibility of conflict. Work through the discomfort by learning to appreciate and recognize the value of diverse opinions and approaches. According to Bourke, "research shows that diversity of thinking is a wellspring of creativity, enhancing innovation by about 20 percent. It also enables groups to spot risks, reducing these by up to 30 percent." (Bourke, How to be smarter and make better choices, 2016)

Understanding how your team members think helps reduce those risks. There are a number of ways to get to know your team better. One of the best is through simple personality tests. Small business owners and team leaders often get new insight into how to understand, motivate, and encourage each other with a better understanding of how their team members communicate. The simpler the test, the better. The goal is to understand your team not to psychoanalyze them. (Bolton and Bolton 2009)

There are many tests. Here are a few commonly used:

- DiSC
- Myers Briggs Test
- Bankcode
- Leadership Styles
- Enneagram

Embracing Responsible Turnover

Avoid making turnover personal. Even when you have worked with someone for years you may come to a point where separation is the right thing for a variety of reasons. Often, your team members need to leave to continue to grow their career. Sometimes you need them to leave because they are no longer a fit and/or a match. Things change. The perfect team may not stay perfect forever.

According to an article published by Newsweek, CEO of Shopify Tobias Lütke, sent an e-mail to managers in 2021 stating, "Shopify, like any other for-profit company, is not a family. The very idea is preposterous. You are born into a family. You never choose it, and they can't un-family you. The dangers of 'family thinking' are that it becomes incredibly hard to let poor performers go. Shopify is a team, not a family." (Fung 2021)

Responsible turnover requires:

- Noticing Turnover Red Fags
- Responding to Changing Job Responsibilities
- Creating Opportunities for Innovation
- Offering Budget Savings

Noticing Turnover Red Fags

Too much turnover is bad for business and if you have more than 33 percent turnover in a single year then it would pay to go back and do some research to figure out why. Training is expensive and not something you want to have to do all the time unless it is part of your business model.

Responding to Changing Job Responsibilities

Sometimes turnover is necessary not because employees are stuck but because growth brings change. Small businesses tend to have fewer layers of management. In so many ways, that is beneficial. It equips small businesses with the flexibility and agility they need in the marketplace.

However, as you grow, you may find that team members who were very good at their jobs when you were smaller find themselves less comfortable now. New requirements may be more than they can handle. They may be resistant to more training. They are no longer a fit.

Some team members thrive in an environment of change that invites new people and new ideas and rewards innovation. Other team members may not be as comfortable with change. The job is no longer a match even if it still fits. Understanding that that is likely to happen will help you create a plan to manage the necessary changes when it does. This can be a hard moment.

Opening Opportunities for Innovation

When teams never bring on new members, the level of innovation tends to go down over a few years. Team dynamics tend to start to support doing things the same. New team members bring with them the whole of their past experience.

In that past experience, there may be opportunities for change that will improve the effectiveness and efficiency of your business you do not want to miss. While 33 percent turnover in one year may be bad, it is likely that 33 percent over five years is good. Allowing the natural evolution of turnover benefits your business. New team members reduce complacency and encourage taking steps to increase efficiency.

Offering Budget Savings

Turnover can be essential to maintaining your budget as well. Providing raises as a reward for excellent work is an essential part of keeping your team happy. This arrangement works as long as the pay that you offer is in alignment with your competitors and in keeping with your ability to make a profit.

However, your team members still expect raises even if a raise would put them outside of the industry pay scale for their position. Without turnover, no matter how much you care for them, your staff can become too expensive to ensure the profitability of your organization. If you avoid going over budget and reduce or eliminate raises for people who are at the top of their pay range then you may see that resentment builds up.

When you encourage your team members to grow their careers even if it sometimes means leaving you everyone wins. Embracing sound turnover allows employees to go on to better paying jobs with more interesting opportunities. You can then bring in people with the necessary skills who fill your teams with great innovative ideas at a lower wage.

Taking Action When Someone No Longer Fits

Most of the time, resources deserve an opportunity to improve before being let go. Some states even require that the ensuing detailed three-step process be followed except when your resource abandons a job, exhibits behavior that is violent, causes a valid safety concern, and/or violates the law. You must protect your business by having a documented process for termination.

Consider this process after determining it fits with the laws and regulations that govern your business.

Step One—Verbal Warning

1. Document the details of the upcoming warning and prepare and a notice that indicates a verbal warning has been received.
2. Meet with your resource providing a detailed verbal warning that includes KPIs your resource is expected to meet within a specified probation period, usually 30, 60, or 90 days.
3. Ask your resources to sign the notice agreeing that the verbal warning was received.
4. Make notes about anything significant that occurred in the conversation including a refusal to sign the notice you presented.
5. Place the documents in the resource's file.

Table 8.1 Written Warnings

If	Then
No infractions occur during the probationary period and the stated KPIs have been met	The matter is resolved
New infractions occurred or the KPIs were not met	Continue to Written Warning

Note: Refusing to sign a verbal warning (Table 8.1) is an infraction.

Step Two—Written Warning

1. Use the document that you made to support your verbal warning to create an Agreement to Improve Performance written warning within a specified time probation period, usually 30, 60, or 90 days.
2. Sit down with your resource in a private place.
3. Have the resource read and sign the Agreement to Improve Performance.
4. Go over the agreement to make sure your team member understands all requirements.
5. Make notes about anything significant that occurred in the conversation including a refusal to sign the agreement you presented.

Step Three—Termination

1. Prepare a Severance Agreement which includes any compensation you may be offering and details about when payment will be made.

Table 8.2 Written Warning

If	Then
No infractions occur during the probationary period and the stated KPIs have been met	The matter is resolved
New infractions occurred or the KPIs were not met	Continue to Termination

Note: Refusing to sign a verbal warning (Table 8.2) is an infraction.

2. Ask your attorney to review the agreement to make sure you are in compliance with all laws and regulations that govern your business.
3. Arrange for security to be present if necessary.
4. Meet with the resource one more time to say goodbye being calm but firm providing no details about why the situation has come to this to avoid confrontations.
5. Gather access keys or cards along with any work materials and equipment from your resources and/or agree to have items turned over to a courier at a specific date and time.
6. Ask your departing resource to read and sign the Severance Agreement.
7. Place the agreement in the resource's file.
8. Add any pertinent notes including a note stating your resource refused to sign if necessary.

Changing Operational Capacity

The business that supports your drive to build and launch a successful opportunity to grow capacity must grow as well. Grow capacity with better systems that support increased efficiency, new resources that support greater effectiveness, and improved skills that support increased aptitude. Creating an environment that supports capacity growth creates a balance between rising customer demands and your ability to supply high-quality products and/or services. Use best practices to build a foundation that creates the balance you need to grow.

Small businesses that are successful at expanding capacity have these things in common:

- Regular Support
- Predictable Metrics

- Vibrant Dash Boards
- Flawless Financials
- Repeatable Processes
- Clear Procedures
- Managed Change
- Strong Teams
- Healthy Culture
- Useful Meetings

Regular Support

Corporations and larger companies have boards and C-Suite teams of executives to leverage as support. Small business owners often report feeling alone with no one to objectively listen and provide guidance. Utilize any combination of business advisors, peer groups, consultants, fractional leaders, accelerators, incubators, or online business communities available as your support network.

Reach out for guidance knowing you have the option to only use the suggestions that make sense to you. Asking for opinions does not give away autonomy. You are still the final decision maker. Needing support does not equate to being weak or unprepared. Sun Trust studied high performing businesses to see what they had in common. They found "that high growth businesses report that they seek advice and guidance from peers and professionals at a much higher rate than other businesses." (Sun Trust Team 2017)

Predictable Metrics

Metrics are of course the KPIs you set for your business. Use your metrics as a driving force to influence behavior designed to support attaining your long-term goals. Use predictable metrics to measure not just the numbers that predict performance, but also the effectiveness of processes to produce the change necessary to drive growth.

Take a look at the growth you predicted in your quarterly and annual goals. Break up those predictions into monthly KPIs that can be included on your dashboard. For example, you may want to measure growth in revenue month after month compared with the previous year to make sure you are hitting your target. You may also want to measure a percentage increase in customers or decrease in refunds to meet predicted goals. If you are carrying debt, you may want to watch the predicted reduction in your balance(s) as well to be sure you are on track. Your predicted KPIs are unique to your goals.

Measure process improvement as well. Make sure the foundation you built remains solid. Measure the predicted outcomes you expected to gain with your process improvements such as more professional communication, reduced internal conflict, or more efficient preparation. Sometimes team members comply with a change at the beginning and then slip back into old habits. Use operational assessment audits, team member reviews, and follow-up to measure your team member's compliance with best practices over time. Once your standard operating procedures are set with agreed upon processes and procedures, predict and expect no less than 100 percent compliance.

Flawless Financials

Most entrepreneurs today use online accounting tools. EVEN if you are in an industry that does not require you to have computer skills and you have no desire to acquire them, it pays to keep your books using an accounting program. A bookkeeper or CPA can help you set up or clean up your financials if necessary.

Financial best practices require:

- Financial Software
- Operational Budgets

Financial Software There was a time when businesses used ledgers entered with pencils before spreadsheets such as Excel or Goggle Sheets. That time has gone by now. Many businesses still use spreadsheets, but that time is passing too. The accuracy and flexibility of free and low-cost software makes maintaining accurate financial records easier than ever before. Bookkeepers and careful accountants want to prepare financial reports easily and more accurately using standardized accounting software. Additionally, most small business owners and leaders like you appreciate the ease of pressing a button to get a wide variety of financial reports without paying someone for hours of work as well.

Financial software has many benefits:

- Prevents simple mathematical errors
- Eases tax preparation
- Provides useful reports
- Reduces data entry duplication

Choose your financial software carefully. Selection criteria might include:

- Cost
- Easy access
- Ease of use
- Easy interface
- Features and functions important to you

Operational Budgets Budgeting for your projects and opportunities is important. Budgeting for your entire business is even more so. Your project and opportunity budgets work best when they roll up to your operational budget. Bankers and investors want to know that you know the costs of running your business and you are financially prepared for unexpected surprises. Entrepreneurs who maintain budgets are more likely to be profitable.

Start your budget based on your history of spending if you have one. If you do not, then start with industry standards and tweak the budget to mirror your expectations. Predicting your costs often helps in setting healthy sales goals and making responsible hiring and purchasing decisions.

Budgets do not just predict costs. When you compare your monthly and yearly budgets to your actuals you see how close your predictions came to reality. Often, in the beginning, your predictions may be wrong. At this point, many give up thinking budget do not work. However, understanding those differences improves your accuracy and helps you build better budgets for your future.

Building Credibility

Establishing credibility is one of the key ways that businesses build trust among the purchasing community. It goes without saying that the better your reputation, the easier it becomes to sell your products and/or services. Build credibility by doing the following:

- Utilize Your Website
- List Your Business on Dunn and Bradstreet
- Take Advantage of Longevity
- Leverage Shortcuts

Utilize Your Website

Making your business easy for customers to find is the first step to building credibility. EVERY business should have a website as has been said before. Most businesses want to be found on one or more social media sites. It does not matter if your customers find you from your website or not. Having a website that can be viewed establishes you as a legitimate business. If you do not have a website, take steps to get one today.

Take Advantage of Longevity

The first three-to-five years of any business can be the most tenuous. Customers want to know that you plan to hang around. Your ability to hang around is proven by the ability you have shown to be around. It makes sense then, that the longer you are in business providing good reliable products and/or services, the more people trust you. Referrals tend to grow exponentially after 3, 5, and 10 year business anniversaries. If you have been in business a while, it pays to make that well known.

List Your Business on Dunn and Bradstreet

A Dunn and Bradstreet listing helps establish the longevity of your business. Good scores and ratings help establish your creditworthiness and stability. Your account also establishes you as a unique entity. Your account or DUNS (data universal numbering system) number may be required to apply for government grants or to receive government contracts. If you are not listed on Dunn and Bradstreet, get listed now. If you are not sure whether you are listed, search for your account DUNS number at www.dnb.com/duns-number/get-a-duns.html.

Leverage Shortcuts

There are several shortcuts to credibility. Take advantage of as many as you can. Consider:

- Franchises
- Alignment with Investors
- Partnering with Mature Businesses

Franchises

One shortcut to obtaining credibility for very young businesses is to align yourself with a more mature business. New franchisers can do that by using the franchise start date and not their own when advertising. You may not have been in business long but your franchisor is providing you with their hard-earned wisdom and experience. You paid to take advantage of that experience in your franchise fee. For example, when you see a new burger franchise such as McDonalds, you are not likely to wonder if the owner is new or the restaurant is well run. The franchisor purchased the McDonalds creditability and took advantage of the training that supports the chain's reputation for consistent delivery.

Aligning With Investors

Another shortcut to credibility can be found by aligning with a well-known investor. Investors that have a lot of name recognition with the public are considered by many to be wise about who to back. If someone with experience is backing you, then often times customers will expect that you have been well capitalized and well vetted. This shortens the timeline you need to build creditability.

Partnering With Mature Businesses

Working as a subcontractor is yet another way to get credibility early. You may not have the reputation and longevity to get a big contract but someone does. Serving as a sub often allows you to build relationships with customers who otherwise might not be interested in speaking to you at all. Adding projects to your business resume that others recognize and respect can improve your RFPs and RFQs. Always be sure to be clear that you were a sub though because clearly stating your involvement is essential to maintaining your credibility.

Adding Value Through Documentation

The value of good documentation cannot be overstated. If you have not been convinced yet, ask yourself: if you could find out the secret to adding 15 to 25 percent to the valuation of your company, would you want to know it? Would you follow the steps even if it might take some time? If you could do one thing that would make your company more stable and resilient during periods of high growth or great change, would you do that even if it too some time? The path to consistent best practices comes through documentation.

The truth is that your business operations either encourage growth or discourage it. The secret to encouraging growth is so apparent it is often overlooked. The answer is simple and when done right easy.

Constant Process Improvement
Using
Accurate and Useful Documentation

This is as true for startups as for global corporations. Bankers, VCs, and potential purchasers know that documented businesses who focus on constant process improvement are worth more than businesses that do not. Businesses that use regular operational audits, well-drawn workflows, and step-by-step procedures as a way of building best practice–based standard operating procedures are prized. This is not the same as writing a manual and sticking it in a desk somewhere never to be opened again.

Documentation has been used for years as a way of increasing value and managing change. Regularly updated standard operation procedures used as a part of constant process improvement create the opportunity to grow capacity. Constant process improvement is based on the theory that things change and as a result we change. If we are paying attention, we can change for the better.

There are many benefits. Here are just a few:

- Reducing Risk
- Creating Accountability
- Benefiting From Internal Experience
- Finding Gaps
- Making Positive Change Faster
- Increasing Business Value

Reducing Risk

Bankers and VCs hate risk. When your operations are carefully documented, your business is at less risk from the loss of a key person. Key people include business owners such as you, leaders, technical experts, and single sources of valuable information. Knowledge stored in someone's head is knowledge easily lost. A key person is someone that would be hard to replace and that if suddenly lost because of illness, injury, job change, or life changes your business would need time to recover. Documenting all of your processes greatly increases the probability you can keep going without the loss of a key person becoming a crisis.

Creating Accountability

When you and your impacted resources agree your documentation is correct, you agree on a standard. Your team members can more easily be held accountable if they deviate. Conversations about performance become easier. There can be only two reasons an employee does not follow procedure. Your team member either did not follow the procedure or the procedure is wrong, and it needs to be updated. There is no room for debate. Less debate equals more harmony.

When you routinely hold your team members accountable according to the standards agreed, you set expectations that procedures must be followed. Team members are less likely to drift back into bad habits. Necessary changes are more likely to be discussed, agreed upon, and then properly documented. Changes are no longer made in a vacuum without regard to others who may be impacted.

Benefiting From Internal Experience

Many times, as your team members are doing the same task over and over again, they eventually discover steps that make them better at their job. This is the theory behind Total Quality Management developed by W. Edwards Deming PhD which later led to Six Sigma and lean manufacturing sometimes called Just In Time (JIT).

Deming said, "Improve constantly and forever every process for planning, production, and service." He believed that if you ask the best people in your company why they are the best, they will tell you. If you do not ask, they often keep it to themselves. When you and your best team members write down the steps to being best you shorten the learning curve for everyone who comes along later. Everyone becomes better together. (Deming 1986)

Finding Gaps

The very act of committing to a process by documenting it in a workflow with the supporting step-by-step procedures helps you find the gaps in your processes that are inhibiting efficiency and discouraging growth. Workflows especially help identify where handoffs could be tighter and communication better so that every team gets the opportunity to show up at their best. Improving procedures so that team members know how to prepare and when to start can lower overall frustration and reduce costs associated with late delivery and mistakes.

Even very small companies with one or two people benefit from writing procedures. If you take time off, have an emergency, or have to grow very quickly the time you took may save your business. Additionally, writing down the steps to procedures you do infrequently saves time. For example, if you renew a license or certification only once a year, chances are you may not remember how next time. Taking time to write down the steps saves you from having to figure out the process again every year.

Making Positive Change Easier

Change happens. When you are in charge of change it is more likely to be beneficial to you. Businesses that survived the Pandemic were able to pivot quickly. Those who used workflows and procedures to document standard operating procedures could explore and get feedback about their new procedures for the pivot first. They were better able to uncover gaps in their pivot plans BEFORE they became costly mistakes.

Use your documentation to explore multiple options in times of change. Pick the option most likely to meet your needs with less stress and risk. Make your team more resilient by using your documentation to build a process of continual improvement. Teams that operated using the concept of continuous improvement could look at the Pandemic pivot as just another opportunity to do better in changing circumstances. Those kinds of teams are the most resilient.

Increasing Value

Bankers, investors, and purchasers, especially VCs, know that small businesses often have team members and especially team leaders and owners who wear many hats and have little back up. They know that it is likely that you and your leaders may walk away during a transition. For this reason, increasingly they discount the value of companies that cannot prove that the organization is well run by the documentation they keep.

In fact, it is a well-known strategy used by VCs to find an under documented company and purchase it for a discount. These VCs know they can spend a year documenting the processes which will lead to improving them. When the business is efficient, effective, and well-documented, they can sell it and take the added value as profit for themselves.

Grow Capacity With Templates

Templates work because they take advantage of repeatable processes. Most anything that is done in a business has been done by someone else at some time. Every report, proposal, and form has been created in one version or another. Templates save an enormous amount of time and energy because they reduce the amount of time it takes to create a document.

Using Templates

Avoid recreating the proverbial wheel. Templates are the simplest form of automation. Use templates to create consistency that helps ensure better quality and improved performance. Standardization reduces errors. The Internet is full of free and low-cost templates that can be used at little or no costs. Sites such as CapacitySquared.net have even gathered many of the standard work week templates in one place for your convenience.

How do you know when you need a template? Anytime that you find yourself gathering, writing, or presenting the same information over and over again it is likely that a template would save time.

There are a variety of ways to use templates:

- Formats
- Checklists, Reports, and Forms
- Information Chunks
- Responses

Format

Many documents such as user documentation, training materials, presentations, proposals, quotes, and so on, are often presented on a regular basis. Formatting these documents only once in a template to save time and improve quality and consistency. Corporations use templates as part of branding. If you get a document from IBM, you know by the look and feel it came from IBM. Brand your business with your own templates.

Help your customers and partners recognize your work right away. Standardize presentations using templates with the same theme and style. Work to present the same information or same type of information to multiple customers is greatly reduced when a slide deck comes with the standard topics and order already laid out. Although some or all of the detail may have to be customized, the template topic flow helps ensure that key points are not forgotten.

Checklists, Reports, and Forms

Standardizing checklists, reports, and forms makes sure that the information required can easily be gathered and found by multiple team members. Being consistent is even more important when your documents are seen by your customers and clients. Consistent documents also help create professional credibility no matter how insignificant the document appears on the surface.

Visual repetition builds your brand. Starting with the work 50 percent to 75 percent done allows your team to quickly capture the information that is unique to your customer or client. It also reduces the amount of time it takes to get repetitive work done.

Information Chunks and Template Responses

Pieces of information your company provides over and over again on forms, in proposals and quotes, on applications, in e-mails, and so on, can become templated responses. Information such as your company description does not or a least should not change from response to response. Why rewrite it over and over again? Instead, save your responses so the information can be copied and pasted instead of recrafted ensuring consistency and quality.

Store templated responses in a common repository such as Drop-Box, Google Docs, or SharePoint making it easier to delegate the work of responding as well. Using the responses reduces the monotony that often leads to burnout. Team members who understand how to use templated responses become more productive as well. A well-crafted response to a frequently asked questions (FAQ) helps team members respond professionally even when they are frustrated, stressed, or overloaded. Many team members start to use the written responses verbally which shortens the amount of time it takes for a new team member to sound professional and informed. You may be surprised at how easily templated responses are adopted.

A museum implemented template responses to questions that were regularly e-mailed to shipping department team members. The same questions came even though there was a FAQ site on the Intranet available to all museum employees. Knowing that shipping antiquities was often much more complex than standard B2B shipments, the team wanted to ensure the information provided was accurate, consistent, and professional. Because of this, e-mails were sometimes delayed because the questions had to be forwarded to a team expert for a response.

E-mail templates were the answer. Any team member even a temporary could use the templates to provide an accurate and reliable response consistent with information that might already be published in FAQs immediately. The templates shortened response time increasing the perception that the shipping team was competent, professional, and reliable among museum employees.

How do you know when to create a template response? If you have provided the exact same information more than three times in one year, then it is likely to be requested again and again. If you save your answer in an information chunk as a templated response and you do not use it again, you can easily delete it from your library later.

Taking Advantage of Automation

Automation may come in the form of software, hardware, or both. Adair Turner Senior Fellow at the Institute of New Economic Thinking in a lecture at John Hopkins reported, "Everything is going to be eventually automated. As a relation to automation the question is when not if." All businesses have some functions in common and automation of these common functions is the new norm in the 21st century. Most industries have common practices within the industry as well where standardization through automation saves time and money. (Turner 2018)

Automated tools offered as cloud applications or desktop software save time and labor while helping to make sure the information needed to run your business is available in real time. Software enforces best practices. The steps that it takes to enter data or to use the application create the procedures that your team must follow. Additionally, most software reduces errors by checking the data as it is entered. Data such as phone numbers, social security number, addresses, and so on, must be entered in the correct format to be accepted. Automation often creates transparency as well. Everyone granted access can see the data. This allows your team members to proactively step up to create better more efficient processes.

Mechanical automation changed the world beginning with the industrial revolution. Machine automation is not new. Its benefits in efficiency and standardization are well known. Today, robots and Artificial Intelligence (AI) are bringing a new revolution.

Many are calling the 21st century the Robotic Age. Innovative robotic pricing was for a long time outside the budget of most small businesses. This is no longer true. Robotic arms do everything from putting stuff in jars, flipping hamburgers, and accomplishing specialized very repetitive tasks. Robots are best at mundane tasks. However, they do not handle unpredictable variables well. A robot can attach a screw at a certain angle and depth every time. It cannot typically adjust if the hole is sometimes one centimeter to the left or two centimeters to the right. The hole has to be in the same pace every single time.

Robots do not burnout, take vacations, or need benefits. Consider robotics if you can pay for a reliable robotic solution for less than the cost of an employee including benefits and taxes over the life of the machine. For example, if you are considering a robotic tool that you expect to be reliable for five years, you need only do the math to make a decision. If a robotic tool costs $25,000 to buy and another $10,000 to learn to use that is a lot of money. However, if an employee costs you $30,000 per year and a robotic tool can do the same work as two employees you save $25,000 the first year. Assuming you do not plan to give raises, over the next four years you save $60,000 per year or $240,000.

AI may however be the biggest change in the 21st century. AI applications gather and sort data much faster than humans. The software rapidly repeats learned processes. AI cannot think on its own. It has to be told what to do and then it practices doing the task over and over until it gets it right. For example, if an AI application looks for red cars it might first pick out colors related to red such as pink, orange, and purple. After being told pink is not red, orange is not red, and so on, over and over again, the application "learns red." After the application knows the color red, it can look at traffic camera video to find and count red cars. When AI is good at counting red cars, it can start to make predictions such as how often a red car might drive by in an hour.

AI becomes particularly good at yes, it matches, or no, it does not. For this reason, AI can do many repetitive tasks such as "learn" the predictable answers to standard questions making unmanned chat boxes useful to support your customers. AI performs research better and faster than humans as well. This has real benefits for research. Some hospitals are beginning to use AI to predict possible diagnosis. However, it takes a human to decide when a diagnosis actually fits based on the unique symptoms of a patient. AI does not have any ability to think creatively.

Use AI to free up your team members when it makes sense such as providing online customer support. Use predictive analytics to predict the features, functions, and required productivity that will be most popular to your customer. Use it to do data interpretations that predict likely outcome of choices. There may be other uses as well.

Managing Market Changes

What your customers want and need changes over the lifetime of your business. You have probably heard the old axiom that the only things that stays the same is change. Markets change (Figure 8.3). Be prepared to change along with your market for your long-term strategy to work.

Figure 8.3 Marketing Maturity Curves

Consider how markets change:

- Trends
- Niche Opportunities

- New Inventions
- Civil Emergencies
- Regulatory Changes

Trends

Trends shift over time and so where your business fits in a trend cycle is important. These curves often look more like an L than a curve. If your business success is based on a trend, you must be ready with the next trendy opportunity before the fad comes to an end.

Toy companies are often good examples of trend businesses. Consider the fidget spinner. For a year, a fidget spinner was a hot item. Kids and even some adults were entranced with the mesmerizing spin all across the United States. They were hot at least until the next trend came along and then they were left in the bottom of a closet or a drawer.

If your business provides stable goods and services, you still need to be aware of trends that impact their market as well. While these trends happen more slowly, they are important. For example, in 1990 if you wanted something printed then you would go to a printer. By the year 2000, you were much more likely to print from your home or office. Printing businesses struggled but printing was easier and more common, so paper mills flourished and printer manufacturers grew. By the year 2020, the Internet had made the need to print a document rare. Printer manufacturers and paper mills saw their businesses shrink. And so, it goes, you want to know how your business is impacted by the trends that create your marketing maturity curve.

Niche Opportunities

Your market does not always have to be growing to be viable. These are opportunities for small businesses to fulfill a need that may not be growing but will be around for a while. Consider niche markets when you can make a profit from a segment of business a larger competitor may not have any interest in pursuing.

For example, home air conditioning unit manufacturers moved away from using freon at the turn of the century. However, homeowners with freon units still needed them serviced. They did not want to replace units that worked because they ran out of freon. Small servicers who handed freon stayed in business maintaining freon units for more than a decade. This is what marketers call the long tail because the need is greatly reduced but does not go away making the end of the marketing curve look like a tail. These tails create niche markets.

New Innovations

Innovations shift markets. The automobile ended most travel by train in the United States in the 19th century. Electric cars are replacing those powered by fossil fuels. One grows while the other declines.

Civil Emergencies

Emergencies though rare have immediate impact that sometimes cause short-term and sometimes lasting change. The Covid-19 pandemic changed markets overnight as people who easily moved around for work and play sheltered in place. Tech companies that supported remote workers were big winners while restaurants closed by the thousands.

These changes cause immediate disruption. Once they are over, the market that existed to support the disruptions begins to shift back except but may never completely return. In the beginning of the pandemic, face masks were in high demand. After the widespread adoption of vaccinations and the innovation of medication to treat the virus, the face mask need went away. This was a short-term change. However, many workers who quickly adjusted to working from home made a cultural shift. The percentage of workers working remotely went down as offices reopened but not to prepandemic levels. Resources found they liked working from home and were willing to change jobs to avoid the office full-time creating a lasting change.

Regulatory Changes

Few businesses escape regulation. Regulatory changes can be impactful to both products and services. Needs to meet those challenges can create brand new businesses or shutter others that have been around for a long time. Regulated businesses must carefully watch for impending changes to pivot to meet new demands.

For example, manufacturing was in big demand in the United States in the first half of the 20th century. Changes to environmental and pay regulations made manufacturing more expensive over time. Changes to import/export regulations including taxes make moving products around the world more cost effective. Manufacturing began to move offshore and so small businesses that supported manufacturing quickly lost their customers.

Supporting Change Through Culture

Your business has a culture. Anytime you bring a group of people together whose goal is to accomplish something, a culture forms. If you do not conscientiously create your culture, it grows organically. Organic growth can be good or bad. Create and keep the culture you identified you want by conscientiously making sure your desired characteristics are encouraged and nurtured. Use the Culture Quiz regularly to help maintain the culture you want.

Charles and Don Sull PhD, cofounders of CultureX and MIT researchers, concluded that based on results from the MIT SMR/Glassdoor Culture 500 study in 2021, "Knowing what elements of culture matter most to employees can help leaders foster engagement as they transition to a new reality that will include more remote and hybrid work." (Sull 2021)

Here are characteristics that contribute to a healthy culture:

- Respect for others is expected and given sincerely.
- Accountability is built into all processes and systems.
- Honesty is encouraged and rewarded.
- Transparency discourages rumors, politics, and gossip.
- Collaboration is fostered functionally and cross functionally.
- Flexibility throughout the work environment engages possibilities and encourages process improvement even in periods of great change.

- Delegation is done carefully with clear expectations.
- Time is managed wisely.
- Remote and virtual cultural environments are as important as the cultural environment on site.

Healthy cultures must be nurtured. Building a healthy culture takes time and attention. Cultures can shift quickly in times of change. Often, new influences cause conflicts.

For example, Rob Becker did an informal study of anthropology and claimed to have come to a better understanding of how humans communicate. As it turned out, he was also very funny. He would often pair college lecture tours with nights headlining at comedy clubs. His show, Defending the Caveman focused on the difference between male and female cultures.

He explained the friction that sometimes happens when people come together during a lecture at the University of Texas at Dallas. According to Becker, groups develop a culture over time. What is considered polite in one group may not be considered polite in the other. He illustrated his point with the "chip and dip theory of female/male communication." (Becker 1992)

Becker began by telling a story that went something like this. A group of women get together for an evening and they've brought chips and dip with adult beverages. Eventually someone notices that the group is running low on chips. One woman says, "I will go and get more chips." Another woman immediately says, "I'll help you I'll get more dip." A third woman says, "As long as we're doing that we could use more wine. I'll go open a new bottle." Everyone is happy.

A group of men across town are doing the same thing. The men are enjoying their conversation when one notices that the chips are running low. The man says, "We need more chips." Another man replies, "I brought the chips." A third man says, "I just brought everybody a beer." The conversation continues until the group determines who lost the competition and that man gets up to get more chips. Again, everyone is happy.

Within the inner circle of each culture, the norms have been applied. The problem comes when you mix the cultures. Becker went on. The next week both the men and women come together as a larger group to share conversation and adult beverages. This time a woman notices the chips are running low. She says, "I think we need more chips." One of the men immediately replies, "I brought the chips." All of the women simultaneously look at the man and think "what a jerk." (Becker 1991)

What was acceptable in one culture was not acceptable in the other. The rules are unwritten and, therefore, when new people enter a culture, it can be easy to violate the cultural norms without realizing it. When shifts happen, the culture must adjust, or it will become toxic with judgments of right and wrong that often go unspoken.

Some cultures are more formal than others. The culture of a legal office will most likely be different than the culture of a social media company. Neither is wrong. The important thing is that the culture fits the environment and that the people invited into the culture understand the norms and are comfortable within their surroundings. When newcomers can be comfortable within the work environment, they are a match. When they are not comfortable, they will either become unhappy and make others around them unhappy or they leave.

Respect

Teams come in all forms. Your resource may be an employee, a volunteer, or a group of business partners. Regardless team members that get along are more productive. The more respect your team members show each other, the more likely your team is to interact in harmony. Don and Charles Sull reported, "Respect was more important by far than any other category studied based on the MIT SMR/Glassdoor Culture 500." (Sull and Sull 2021)

Use the tips that follow to help sustain an empowering environment for your organization:

- Use proper titles when making introductions
- Avoid giving military style orders
- Ask for what you want so no one has to guess

- Share credit for a job well done
- Ask about workload before handing off more work
- Praise your staff, contractors, and volunteers
- Refrain from office gossip
- Avoid corrections and criticism in public
- Recognize extra efforts
- Do something nice for your team members regularly

Honesty and Integrity

Even large companies struggle when their reputations are called into question Your word is your bond. Whether or not you keep your word is part of your business reputation, damage to your reputation can have a lasting impact.

For example, many years ago a national retailer became widely known for delaying payment to small vendors for up to 120 days outside their agreement to pay. They knew small vendors were unlikely to report to the credit bureau but were likely to experience great hardship when payment is delayed. Although their credit rating was not hurt, news of distressed vendors made it extremely hard to find vendors who would do work with them. Other vendors charged them more to account for the interest charges of paying their resources and expenses while waiting for payment. The cost of saving money by delayed payment became higher than the cost of paying on time.

If you say you are going to pay someone when the job is done, you HAVE to have the money available even if your customer's check does not clear. If you say you will pay when you get paid then as soon as the payment has cleared your account, you must pay as promised.

In the same way, you and your leadership team must keep promises to your team members. If you promise that someone will get a raise, you must make sure that happens. If you promise that certain resources will become available to your employees that will make their jobs somehow better or easier to do, you must be ready to make the investment. If you promise that something will change about your business, you must make that one of your goals.

Transparency

In order to be transparent, an entrepreneur must share facts about the business. Leadership teams must be empowered to be truthful as well. Transparency has risks. If you decide that transparency is important then you have to be transparent even when it is uncomfortable. If you or your leadership team has made promises that you made in good faith, but something has changed, the sooner you tell those who are impacted the better.

What happens when you cannot tell the truth? If you are not comfortable being transparent then you must say that right up front. Sometimes secrets are necessary and may even be forced because of laws or regulations and that cannot be helped. Just know that when secrets are kept, those around you are aware. When you are in the situation, save trust by being transparent about what the situation is and why.

For example, Mark Cuban, the billionaire owner of the Dallas Mavericks often seen on Shark Tank, was the innovator of streaming video on the Internet. When he began, he faced regulatory challenges. He hired resources and started development. However, there was a point where development stalled while regulatory changes were in process. One of his software engineers came to him and said that he did not see the future.

Cuban told him that he was bound by rules and regulations not to provide details and assured the young man if he stayed, it would be worth his while. Cuban was completely transparent that there was a risk but tried to reassure his developer that the risk was being managed. The developer left.

Six months later regulations changed, Cuban was able to launch broadcast.com and then sell it to Yahoo for a huge profit. The resources who stayed were handsomely rewarded. Those who left were not angry with Cuban. He was transparent.

Being transparent does not mean that you share everything with your employees and contractors. Being transparent about the boundaries you face is still transparency.

Collaboration

When your team works better together, your business does more, better, and faster than it did before. Fostering a collaborative environment permits your team members to ask questions and learn from each other. Issues are reduced and productivity increases. When your team members feel free to reach out right away when something goes wrong your business becomes better at solving proems quickly. Team members who are regularly brought together in effective team meetings to collaborate tend to report feeling more valued which reduces turnover, improves efficiency, and reduces costs.

Flexibility

Flexible cultures happen in businesses where change is managed well and issues are easily recognized and continually resolved. Flexible cultures experience less chaos in times of change. The business actually becomes more resilient because team members trust that they can bring up issues knowing risk is managed well. In flexible cultures, people are empowered to be honest.

Time Management

Build a culture that expects efficiency by managing time well. If you or your team members cannot manage to get all the work planned done in a workday on a regular basis then something is wrong. This might exclude seasonal up ticks and predictable deadline pushes, but on average, work should be done in the timeframe expected. When your team knows what is expected, you can hold each other accountable.

If overtime is a day-to-day regular part of your budget, then you must consider what should be done to avoid team member burn out and protect your revenue. Either the plan is wrong, you need more resources, or your resources are not working as efficiently and effectively as they could. All of these issues can be fixed. First, recognize there is a problem. Second, determine what the problem(s) are as quickly as possible. Third, make the necessary corrections.

Be the example of how time is best managed within your organization. If you insist meetings stay on topic, show up on time, meet your deadlines, and focus on your work during work hours your team will expect that they should do the same. You and your leadership team set the standard.

When your resources do not achieve goals, hold them accountable. When your resources DO achieve their goals, celebrate their achievements. Oftentimes, it takes no more than an attaboy in front of the group to encourage others to strive to meet their goals as promised.

Priority Setting

When there is much to be done then it is time to set short-term priorities in alignment with your long-term goals. Your Roadmap to Success provides strategic focus. Focusing on meeting milestones on your long-term plan is another way to prioritize. Another is to realign your efforts based on what needs to be done right now to avoid being overwhelmed by competing priorities.

Use the Eisenhower Matrix pictured below (Figure 8.4) as one tool to help you focus your concentration on what matters. Avoid using this tool to procrastinate. Your long-term and short-term priorities must be given consideration. For example, if one of your goals is to better understand your financials and/or document your business within the next year and those things are important to you, they should show up on your matrix.

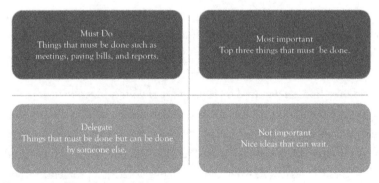

Figure 8.4 Eisenhower Matrix

CHAPTER 9

Maintain

If you really look closely most overnight successes took a long time.

—Steve Jobs

Maintaining Your Business

Once you build your business, you must constantly use best practices to maintain your effectiveness and grow your capacity. Without time and attention, businesses stagnate. Consider the following to protect your investment:

- Risk Management
- Constant Process Improvement
- Effective Meetings

Risk Management

All plans have risks. Recognizing those risks provides a way to mitigate and plan for a response BEFORE a crisis. Once you know the risks you face, prioritize each and do what you can to mitigate each. In some cases, understanding risks creates new strengths and turns threats into opportunities. Decisions become easier to make because the information is readily available. As long as you are a privately held company and your risk management plan includes the key components, it does not need to be elegant. It only needs to be easily understood, followed, tracked, and refined to be worth the time it took you to prepare the plan.

Manage risk using:

- SWOT Analysis
- Risk Assessments

- Audits
- Disaster Recovery Plans

SWOT Analysis

SWOT stands for strengths, weaknesses, opportunities, and threats (Figure 9.1). Use this matrix as a collaborative tool to identify what works for you both internally and externally. Then identify what might impede your growth in the same way. Be open to considering new insights. Often in the midst of identifying risks and threats, new opportunities become apparent.

For example, an internal strength may be how agile you are at adjusting to changes in the market or how quickly you can ship a product after an order. An external opportunity might be how many Requests for Proposals (RFPs) are being posted that match your teams' abilities or your customer's loyalty to your brand making it easier to launch a new product. An internal weakness might be time wasted in unproductive meetings or frequent equipment issues. An external threat might be new competitors or new proposed regulations.

Creating and reviewing a SWOT analysis once or twice a year is a good way to take a step back and see your business from a different point of view. Use the matrix to look at your business as a whole or to examine where you stand in important functional areas such as marketing, sales, and production. Often, your team sees things you do not. Remember to include those impacted in your exercise to get multiple viewpoints.

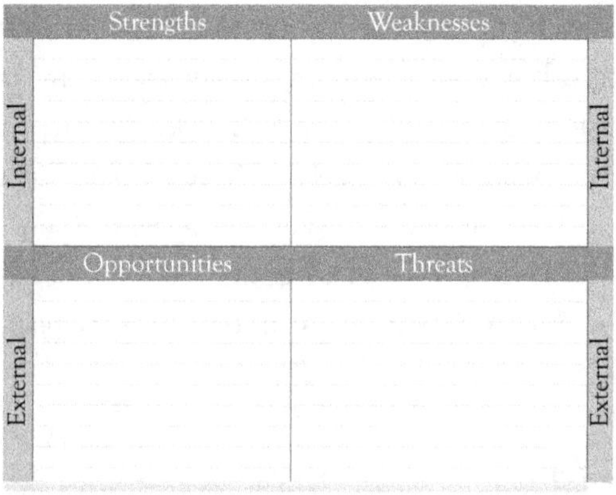

Figure 9.1 SWOT Analysis

Risk Assessments

Every company is impacted by the world around them. There are always internal and external pressures. Understanding your environment often provides a competitive advantage that helps you avoid problems and take advantage of opportunities your competitors might not see. While a SWOT Analysis identifies risks, a risk assessment provides a more in-depth analysis. Some software applications provide a risk assessment tool; however, you can use any spreadsheet program to document and assess your risks as shown in the template below (Table 9.1).

Risk Register

Table 9.1 Risk Register

ID	Description	Related Functions	Category	Impact	Probability	Priority

To determine your risks, ask yourself:

1. What risks do we face?
2. What business functions are impacted?
3. How would I categorize that risk?
   - Safety
   - Interruption
   - Continuity
   - Disruption
4. What is the impact of the risk?
5. What is the probability of facing these challenges?
6. How do we prioritize our mitigation efforts and reduce the risk of the challenge?

Audits

Ask systemic questions about how your business is doing and how it is being run on a regular basis. Doing due diligence on your own organization provides insights you are unlikely to see in any other way. Even knowing that you do not know the answer right now is valuable. Identifying gaps in your understanding of how and why you operate shows you what you are missing. Use your insights to fill those gaps as quickly as possible.

Audits do not have to be done at the same time. It does help though if each one is done at the same time each year. Consider doing one each quarter. Put audits on your calendar so that you have a regular schedule from year-to-year.

Consider the following audits:

- Financial
- Operational
- Project
- Safety

Financial Audits

An annual financial review is a good idea to avoid issues, make sure taxes are properly handled, and better understand how you are using your money. If you leave your financials to your bookkeeper and/or CPA and rarely look at your books, then an annual financial audit is a must. Regular audits ensure your financial records are meeting Generally Accepted Accounting Principles (GAAP), which are best practices for any business. It is essential to understand how your books are being kept.

Regular audits help when applying for loans. Some lenders may require an audit as a part of the application process to validate the financials you present are accurate. Grantors may ask for audits as well to ensure the money given is being used as promised. Audited financials are also important during a sell. Perspective buyers often choose an outside audit firm to do due diligence. Most importantly, routine auditing discourages theft. Theft may be the biggest risk because small businesses are often too small to afford regular oversight and best practices that require separation of duties.

"Private companies and small business rank highest in occupational fraud frequency at 42 percent compared to large corporations, government and nonprofits," according to the Association of Certified Fraud

Examiners 2018 Global Study on Occupational Fraud and Abuse led by Ben Davis, CEO of Certified Fraud Examiners (Davis 2020) Small businesses are most vulnerable to billing scams, payroll schemes, and embezzlement. Financial audits are best handed handled by third-party professionals to keep your business secure.

Operational Audits

Routinely auditing your operations with an Operational Assessment provides you with the opportunity to look at your business from a different perspective. Use these types of audits as a regular team collaboration tool. Give the audit assessment to your leadership team. Ask each team member to do the assessment separately and then they gather to compare answers. This is one way to keep your team leaders on the same page. Clear up any discrepancies before the gaps cause problems. Fill any gaps as quickly as possible.

Project Audits

Project audits of long running projects help ensure that project budgets are being used wisely and best practices are being used. Audits confirm quality standards are being followed and risks are being effectively managed as well. Highly technical audits may require a third-party auditor. Other audits can be performed by you or a team member.

Follow the steps below to conduct an audit.

Step One—Conduct the Audit

1. Review the project scope to be sure the project is in alignment with what was promised.
2. Meet with each team member using a checklist of project standards to determine if standards are being met.
3. Examine issues reports to be sure issues are being captured and promptly resolved.
4. Review action item reports to be sure action items are assigned with deadlines and the deadlines are being met.

5. Interview stakeholders to be sure their expectations are being met.

6. Review the project plan, communication plan, and risk management plan for accuracy and completeness.

7. Examine project documents for quality and thoroughness.

Step Two—Document and Present Findings

1. Document any issues you discovered throughout your audit.

2. Prepare a presentation of your report.

3. Meet with the project team to discuss the results and come up with plans to handle issues appropriately.

4. Add assignments from the review meeting to the appropriate issues or action items report.

5. Follow up to make sure issues and action items have been addressed.

Safety Audit

Every business must be concerned with safety. Keeping your team members safe from physical threats is important. It is just as important to keep your equipment, hardware, and software safe from cybercrimes. Safety audits tend to be very specific to your industry and may be regulated by state and federal agencies.

- Make sure your company data is protected by a firewall.
- Require team members to install and keep virus protection software up-to-date regardless of whether the device is personally owned.
- Include password standards that require industry accepted password protocols in your policies and procedures.
- Be vigilant about requiring timeouts on all devices so screens go dark when the user walks away.
- Ensure any office and buildings you utilize meet building codes.
- Practice fire drills in any location where your team members come together to meet or work.
- Review state and federal regulations on a regular basis to be sure your business operates in full compliance.

- Check with industry associations if necessary to be sure you are following a recommend safety guidelines.
- Use good common sense.

Disaster Recovery Plan

Disasters happen. In the summer of 2021, the *Washington Post* reported that one third of the United States population was recovering from one or more events in an article by Sarah Kaplan and Andrew Ba Tran. Between wildfires, tornados, floods, and hurricanes, millions of small businesses were impacted. All of these things happened during a pandemic. Emergencies happened amid constantly changing regulations and shutdowns.

Having a well-documented, structured plan, you review regularly before disaster strikes allows your team members to begin to mitigate the damage right away. A plan that is easy to find and follow gets your business up and running again much faster. It often helps mitigate losses as well. (Tran 2021)

Disasters require immediate pivots. Preparation is key. Small businesses that routinely manage change using documented processes can change more quickly with less disruption. Use contingency plans you worked out in advance to mitigate your risks. Even the smallest business benefits from taking one day a year to consider what to do if disaster strikes. Many entrepreneurs report that having a plan makes them worry less.

Assess the risks of disasters by answering these questions to be better prepared to face the future regardless of what happens.

- How will you know your team is safe and what will you do if they are not?
- Where is your computing cloud and how has my data and access to software been impacted?
- What if your business is disrupted?
- What will you do if no power is available?
- How will you connect if no cell/phone service/Internet is available?
- Who will check on equipment and building safety?

- Where will you work if a/the building or equipment is destroyed?
- What happens if team members cannot get to the office?
- Who replaces team members who cannot work?
- Who contacts insurance and how?
- How will you mitigate risks?
- How will you recover from losses?

Plans that work have these characteristics:

- Easily found
- Carefully reviewed
- Regularly practiced
- Routinely updated
- Properly Insured

Start by asking these questions:

- How do we face the challenge?
- How do we prioritize the challenge?
- Is the answer short or long?
- Can we provide documentation online vs paper?
- How will we communicate the plan?
- Who will maintain the plan and how often?

Constant Process Improvement

An agile business never stops improving processes. Process improvement becomes a part of the culture when all team members focus on how they can do what they do better. In the fast-paced 21st century world of information and automation, every industry experiences rapid change. Use that change to be more cost effective and efficient.

This does not mean change for changes sake. Change must provide a clear benefit. Too much change can be as harmful as too little. Your teams will grow weary if they feel there is no consistency and no benefit behind keeping up with constant change. Innovation should do one of two things. First, make work easier, better, smarter, and less time consuming. Second, improve the quality of your product or service.

Effective Meetings

People are busy. You want your team members to be busy doing work that adds to your bottom line. Make sure meetings are necessary, focused, and include only those who actually need to be there.

Meeting together is often one of the most expensive things that happen in a work week. You are paying everyone sitting in the meeting and they are focused on the meeting not on other work. Add the hourly cost of each team member meeting and multiply that total by the time spent meeting you determine the real financial cost. Compare the cost to the benefit the meeting provides to determine if meeting is the best use of time.

Small businesses where everyone works together in one office often need fewer meetings than those who have team members working remotely. Everyone overhears what everyone else is doing. In a small office, there are few secrets. However, strategically held and planned meetings reduce communication issues by ensuring everyone is paying attention. They also provide much needed accountability to help team members manage their time and keep their promises. Remote teams must rely on meetings as the best form of vital team communication.

An effective meeting always spreads information in way that is more detailed and accurate than other communication efforts allow such as e-mail, text, or multiple face-to-face conversations. The best way to benefit from the time your team members spend meeting is to make sure that meetings are purpose driven, efficient, and effective.

Effective meetings have these characteristics in common:

- Clear Leader
- Stated Purpose
- Agenda
- Start and End on Time
- Avoid Time Wasters
- Include Meeting Notes

- Document Issues and Action Items
- Tend to be Short
- Include Follow-Up

Clear Leader

The team member who arranges and invites everyone to the meeting is typically the meeting leader. If a team member is creating a meeting for someone else on the team the agenda should include the intended leader's name.

Stated Purpose

There should be a real purpose behind any meeting that can be stated in one sentence.

Agenda

All meetings should have a published agenda that is distributed before the meeting. Often, agendas are included in the description section of a meeting request. Agendas provide a number of benefits:

- Help leaders make sure the meeting stays on topic.
- Clarify the purpose of the meeting.
- Streamline what needs to be covered.
- Encourage suitable time management.
- Allow team members to come prepared which helps avoid delays.

Start and End on Time. Attendees tend to enthusiastically attend and be prepared when they know your meetings do not go on and on. The best way to make sure your team members come to your meetings on time is to start without people who show up late. Team members who showed up on time should never be subjected to a summary of what has happened so far. Hold late team members accountable to catch up on their own. If you need more time, then schedule another meeting. Do not run over your promised end time.

Include Meeting Notes. No matter how important a meeting is, you will not be able to remember exactly what happened a week from now. Take notes. Typically, the meeting leader takes notes but team members may take turns as well or an admin may be pressed into service. Notes need to be detailed enough to document important discussions and decisions.

Document Issues and Action Items. An action item is really just any promise to do a task. Some people like to keep action items and issues listed separately but others choose to combine them. These lists can be kept as a spreadsheet or by using a wide variety of software task applications. However you keep your list, it is important that each item should have an owner, a status, and an expected resolution date.

Tend to Be Short. Most meetings should be short. There are a few exceptions. Brainstorming and planning meetings such as annual goal planning, budget building, or project planning take time. These meetings can last for hours and need to be scheduled when the team members required can be focused over a longer period of time. They may even need to be broken up into multiple sessions.

Keep meetings short by following your agenda and avoiding time wasters. Small talk, birthday celebrations, and sharing of food may be important to your culture. Have gatherings for those activities. Save meeting times for specific agendas. Consider encouraging brevity by having short meetings. If your team members tend to take a lot of time to give reports, hold stand up meetings in a location with no chairs. Most people use fewer words standing than they do sitting down.

There are three ways to handle something that threatens to derail the meeting.

- **Subject is off topic**
  Gently ask your team to return to the agenda and discuss that later.
- **Subject is on topic and requires input from only some of the meeting members**
  Suggest the topic should be tabled and addressed at the end of the meeting when all those not involved can be released.
- **Subject is on topic and requires input from others who are not in the meeting**
  Suggest that should be taken offline and continued in another meeting and add the meeting to the action items.

Include Follow-Up. Meeting follow-up is the most crucial element of success. Just asking team members if they have done what they promised makes it far more likely that you will get a positive result. Asking in a meeting in front of others doubles your likelihood of success.

Useful Reports

Reports do not have to be formal to be valuable. They do have to be written and stored somewhere where easily found should there be a question later. All small businesses need a reporting structure. The key is to make reporting simple, useful, informative, quick, and easy.

Reports are the quickest way to determine if your business is headed in the right direction, your team members are working efficiently and effectively, and issues and roadblocks to success are being quickly resolved and removed.

Reports help everyone remember what agreements and promises were made. People are human and sometimes forget. Having a document to go back to saves time pointing fingers and helps create a culture of harmony.

Consider using these reports to make sure your business is headed in the right direction:

- Operational Dashboards
- Status

- Issues and Action Items
- Sales
- Financial

Operational Dashboards

Dashboards present the key metrics that tell you how the business is doing. The purpose of a dashboard is to provide the key data necessary for good decision making in one easy-to-access report. Entrepreneurs routinely follow financial, sales, and production data. SaaS companies follow monthly recurring revenue along with new and discontinued membership trends closely. Some business leaders also follow social media engagement metrics and customer satisfaction as well. The data important to you is dependent on the type of business you operate and the metrics that are meaningful to you.

Dashboards can be kept in a wide variety of ways. Some businesses use a white board while others use spreadsheets and still others use online tools. Most every management tool includes a dashboard of some kind. However, if your tools do not talk to each other, then online dashboarding may be disjointed and may require manual input. Often, a third-party app can be used to bring your data together in one view.

Before you create your dashboard, be clear about what metrics you want to track. Keep your dashboard simple and easy to understand to be most effective. Only track metrics you care about now.

Follow the steps below to create a dashboard (Table 9.2):

1. Create a list of the metrics that matter.
2. Determine how often you need to see updates.
3. Decide where the numbers come from and how they get on your report.
4. Build your report on a whiteboard, a spreadsheet, or online.

Example Dashboard

Table 9.2 Sample Dashboard

Financial	Production	Social Media
Monthly Rev Cash on Hand AR Turnover AP Turnover MRR Margin Refunds/Returns/Recalls/Churn	On Time Back Ordered Overtime	Followers Gained Lost LinkedIn Twitter Instagram
Sales	**Inventory**	**Customer Satisfaction**
Leads Opportunities Qualified Negotiations Closed Lost	Cost COGS Turnover	Survey Scores

Status Reports

Weekly status reports encourage your team members to plan work. When people get stuck or issues become stickier than first thought, it becomes clear to see. These reports give you the opportunity to step in and provide assistance at the earliest possible moment. Giving your team a way to report progress makes delegation easier as well. When you see that your team members are doing the work you expect with minimal issues, your trust in them is validated.

Reports are best kept simple. No report should take more than 30 minutes to complete.

It can be as simple as:

Office Resources	Field Technicians
Accomplished this Week	Calls made
In Process	Recalls
Planned	Notes
Issues	Issue

Figure 9.2 Status Report templates

Benefits

Work Planned moves to In Process and then Accomplished when work is going well. Reporting how work is coming along reinforces deadlines and encourages efficiency. When things do not go according to plan, the reasons become clearer. Bottlenecks become more apparent. Staff overload becomes more obvious. Issues can be raised and tracked.

Similarly, field status reports provide valuable insights. When work planned moves to work accomplished with fewer issues, your customers and clients are happy. Recall numbers remain negligible compared with number of first calls when work is done right the first time. Notes make responding to complaints and maintaining customer relationships simpler.

Reported issues do not get forgotten. Issues tend to move from Open to Resolved quickly. If not, you have a red flag that suggests your resource may need help or support. Routinely responding with questions or praise lets your resources know their reports matter. Regular recognition improves team member engagement motivating workers. According to CEO of People Element, Chris Coberly, "Increased employee engagement results in reduced turnover, improved productivity, better customer retention, stronger financial health, and most importantly, happier employees." (Coberly 2021)

Sales Reports

Depending on the pace of your business, you may want daily, weekly, or monthly reports that roll up to your quarterly report. Quarterly reports then of course roll up to annual reports. Sales reports may attract a variety of metrics. The key metrics entrepreneurs care about tend to be sales funnel numbers, status, revenue gained, and revenue lost. Often, lost revenue comes in the form of cancelations, refunds, recalls, or returns. These reports highlight what is going well and raise early red flags when problems arise.

Financial Reports

The same reports that were important to your banker are important to you. Make sure these reports are easy to retrieve. Make sure you understand them. Set time on your schedule to review them every month.

- Cash Flow
- Balance Sheet
- Income Statement
- Budget
- Forecast
- Monthly Recurring Revenue (SaaS)

Accountability Measures

The ability of your team to work when you are not around directly correlates to the value of your business. If your business falls apart unless you hover over your team members, then your absence due to purchase, illness, or any other reason is a giant risk to the viability of your organization. Worker autonomy is essential to growth. One of the ways purchasers, investors, and bankers determine whether entrepreneurs have built a resilient company is by asking owners when and how often they vacation.

These are the characteristics that are important in a business that has a culture of accountability:

- Safe Confession
- Strong Policies and Procedures
- Reliable Standards
- Clear Deadlines

Safe Confession

You may have heard it said that confession is good for the soul. It is also good for a healthy business culture. People need to be able to confess to a mistake so that the mistake can be quickly rectified. When people are afraid to be transparent, mistakes may be hidden in ways that cause a lot of harm to a growing company.

Strong Policies and Procedures

Good policies and procedures set expectations and guidelines for how your team members operate when working on your behalf. A Policies and Procedures guide, also sometimes known as an Employee Handbook, documents guidelines of behavior expected for your employees, key contractors, volunteers, and partners. This guide outlines the expectation and code of conduct for all resources. Policies and procedures are essential for even very small businesses of three people because these guidelines set a baseline for acceptable behavior.

Hold anyone who falls outside the agreed norms of behavior accountable. Reward those who go above and beyond. The larger your organization, the more important an Employee Handbook becomes because it is the first step in documentation should you need to separate someone who is not meeting your expectations. Expectations help you avoid accusations of favoritism, sexism, racism, and so on. Your policies and procedures provide a baseline to be sure all employees are treated fairly.

Each team member given a handbook must review and sign a document agreeing to follow the guidelines they read. Once signed, you have an agreement that helps your team members understand the behavior you expect. The agreement also protects your company should someone act outside of accepted best practices or violate local, state, or federal laws and regulations. Documented policies and procedures are part of the "Book of Your Business" that helps to show the real value of your organization.

If you do not know where to start, begin with a template. There are many free and low-cost templates online. Take care to customize your guide to meet your needs. A standard template is often not enough. Make sure your guide follows a local, state, and federal guidelines.

Standards

Most people want to do a good job. Standards help. Standards apply to everything you do. While many standards are about profit and loss and are designed to make a business efficient and effective, others are about safety and security. Still others ensure regulatory compliance.

Use standards consistently to ensure that materials, products, processes, and services are fit for their purpose. Industry-accepted standards are available for almost all businesses through trade associations, industry-specific regulations, and standard certification organizations such as

International Organization for Standardization (ISO). You may want to create your own that are more precise to your organization.

Deadlines

Deadlines create urgency. Busy people tend to focus on what is most important. Your team members do not tend to make promises cannot keep. However, procrastination is a common human trait. If your team members know they have only a certain amount of time to take action, they become much more likely to do what they promised.

Follow up to be sure deadlines are met. Without the follow-up, team members may procrastinate or even forget what they promised to do. Even more likely, as time goes by the understanding of what was promised will grow fuzzy and the action to take will be less clear. Follow-up reinforces your expectation that your team members must keep their promises. Sometimes however, things do change or the effort to complete the action item or resolve the issue is more complicated than first thought.

Follow-up need not be difficult. Make follow-up the last part of any regularly scheduled meetings such as sales meetings, status meetings, and work planning meetings. One off meetings still need action items and issues documented if there are issues to be resolved. Use software programs that help by to automate reminders and help keep your team on track.

Understanding Your Financials

There is one thing that is very important to understand whether you have been in business a long time or you are starting tomorrow. If you want to have a healthy business, you must be profitable at some point. If your business is not making a profit today, that does not mean that you should quit.

Just like opportunities sometimes require an investment phase, your business may require one too. However, and this is the most crucial point, you must be able to predict the point at which you will become profitable. It does not matter if you are passionate about what you do.

Successful entrepreneurs avoid passion about their business turning into an expensive hobby.

Your financials are not just important when you are pursuing a new opportunity, deciding to get a loan, or when you want to sell your business. Your financials are important because the numbers tell you about the health of your business.

You do not have to be good at numbers. There are any number of financial software options you can use to make accounting easier from spreadsheets to accounting. Applications such as Excel, Google Sheets, Wave, Quicken, Zero, and Sage50Cloud to name a just a few can be used to create those all important financial reports that help you stay on track. You as the leader of your business must make sure the numbers get in accurately by looking at key reports.

Building Credit

All businesses do better when they are creditworthy. Being creditworthy is not the same thing as being in debt. Even if you do not care about being bankable, being creditworthy is important. Individuals get better deals on a multitude of things such as insurance, car loans, and mortgages if they show that they are responsible with money. It is the same for businesses. Businesses that are creditworthy are better able to negotiate contracts, attract investment, buy insurance, and get loans. However, access to credit has been historically more difficult for minority and women owned businesses.

Patricia Greene PhD, founding member of the Diana Project and former head of the Women's Bureau at the U.S. Department of Labor, studied access to capital for women in business. The Diana Project won the International Award for Entrepreneurship and Small Business Research in 2007. Greene states, "The women of the Diana Project wrote Clearing the Hurdles: Women Building High Growth Businesses quite a few years ago. The reasoning behind the title was that all businesses face similar types of hurdles, but those hurdles too often are set at different heights for women, and minority, business owners. Access to capital is certainly one of those hurdles." (Greene 2021)

Credit History

Build a credit history as quickly as you can responsibly do it. Getting turned down for credit does not help your situation though. Be sure you understand the criteria used to determine acceptance before you apply.

Avoid using all your credit even if you think you need to do so. This can be the most confusing aspect of credit ratings. Your credit rating goes up when you use your credit and make payments over time. However, it goes down if you appear to be relying too much on credit and not enough on revenue. That can be hard to determine and so lenders use the percentage of credit you use as a rule. Credit ratings go up when you have access to money, but it appears that you are doing so well you do not need to use all of it. If you stay under 50 percent usage at any given moment as a rule you should be credit worthy.

On Time Payments

Make more than the minimum payment. Create a schedule of payments you can reasonably afford and stick to them. Not only will the schedule help you plan for your financial future, but it shows lenders and investors that you are a good risk.

Getting Help

The good news is that help is available should you need it, often at little or no cost to you. Government-sponsored programs such as the SBA and SBDC provide business advisors to help you understand your financials. Some colleges and universities offer free student-led support in their accounting programs providing accounting services which provide students with real-life experience. Accelerator and incubator programs often include a segment on financials as well and may provide business advisors who often help owners sort out their financials.

Understanding Financial Terms

Like all industries, the banking industry has its own language with its own acronyms that can be confusing if you do not have a financial background. Understanding the language can be the first step in getting past financial report intimidation. Here are key terms you want to know.

Cash Flow

Sometimes called Operating Cash Flow or Cash on Hand, this is the money you have on hand to meet your day-to-day expenses such as payroll, rent, inventory, and so on, each month. Cash flow can come from a variety of sources including investments, loans, and grants. Eventually, though, every entrepreneur wants a positive cash flow that comes from income. When you hear or read "Cash is King," this is what is meant.

AR

Accounts Receivable is the money you take in every month from payments owed to you.

AP

Accounts Payable is your short-term debt or the money you have promised to pay for goods and services you received.

Aging

The amount of time it takes for invoices to be paid to you. Aim for no more than 30 days. Business that wait a long time to get paid are riskier than those who get paid more quickly for obvious reasons. Bankers worry about what might happen if your business customer falls behind or worse files bankruptcy making it hard for you to get paid.

Break Even

Point at which the revenue from an investment is equal to the costs of the investment or when calculated for your business the point when company costs are equal to income generated.

Earnings

Business profits which bankers and investors view in a variety of ways:

- **EBT**—Earnings before taxes
- **EBIT**—Earnings before interest and taxes
- **EBITDA**—Earnings before interest, taxes, depreciation, and amortizations

GP

Gross Profit Margin calculated by subtracting cost of goods sold (COGS) from net sales. Multiplying the answer by 100 gives you the margin in a percentage.

Net

Net Profit Margin calculated by dividing net profit by total revenue and multiplying the answer by 100. Multiplying the answer by 100 gives you the margin in a percentage.

Net Worth

Sometimes referred to as owners'/shareholders' equity or book value which is determine net worth by calculating the total of all assets minus the total of all liabilities.

Owners' Draw

Money taken from the business for personal use that is not part of a salary.

ROI

Return on investment measured by your net income divided by the initial capital cost. The higher the ratio the better the return.

Working Capital

Sometimes referred to as owners'/shareholders' equity or book value determined by net worth. Calculate current assets minus the current liabilities. Current assets are assets that provide a value within a year such as inventory waiting to be sold.

Insurance for Resilience During Growth

Get connected. Isolation is one of the biggest issues that face business owners. Create a support system so you never have to again feel isolated and alone because relationships matter. Reach out for the advice and help you need. Offer the same to others. Connections make you stronger.

Groups available may include the following:

- Advisory Board
- Online Communities
- Support Groups
- Chambers
- Networking Groups
- Bankers

Advisory Board

An advisory board is just what it sounds like, a group of people with expertise in their field willing to offer you strategic advice. Board members test your leadership decisions against best practice principles, offer expertise you may not have, and may help you make connections you need for success. Board members may meet with you together in regularly scheduled quarterly or annual meetings or independently as your need arises depending on what works best for your business. Sometimes board members volunteer, other are paid a stipend, and other are given a gift of appreciation that reflects their contributions once a year.

Online Communities

Communities where Small Business owners and the resources who support them gather to grow capacity fraction by fraction can protect business owners from the isolation that is sometimes inherent with growing a business. These communities have a passion for small businesses whether they operate B2B, B2C, and/or B2G. They feel compelled to assist owners who work so hard. They want owners to be successful and can step up by helping small business owners and team leaders more easily, effectively, and efficiently connect to their future team leaders, team members, and customers.

Targeted cloud communities understand that a small business community stands stronger together. Participating in communities with the right connections and support can help all members grow the capacity to do and be more. These communities such as capacitysquared.net provide a place for members to support each other in an agreement to assist all members so they can all prosper. Memberships are generally very low cost but the ultimate goal of a good community is to support members in meeting their end goals.

Support Groups

Groups such as Entrepreneurs Organization, Vistra, or Score gather business leaders online or in person in peer-to-peer groups. These groups have a wide range of fees and may have qualifications such as a minimum revenue or number of years in business. Some members find the support of these organizations extremely beneficial. They say they are worth every penny while others find the investment did not help them grow. It is important to get references from current and former members of any organization that requires a large fee to join or stay connected to help ensure this type of investment in your future is worthwhile. Finding the right group and becoming actively involved can assist you in getting key introductions to potential customers and suppliers that build your credibility. You just need to be sure you found the right group.

Chambers

Chambers of Commerce can be local, regional, or national. The chamber's entire job is to help business members grow their businesses through better connections to the community, other members, and potential customers. The type of chamber that is most beneficial will be determined by the type of business you own.

Small business owners who are active in trades often report that membership in local chambers increases the number of referrals they receive each year. Referrals build credibility because everyone wants to do business with someone they trust. Trust can be referred. A recommendation from someone you have done business with in the past to a potential customer increases the probability of getting the opportunity to bid on work. Potential customers are more likely to buy from someone who is not a complete unknown.

Networking Groups

Networking groups such as C Suite or Business Networking International provide a community of business owners and leaders the opportunity to connect for the expressed purpose of supporting each other success. Good groups make business support their number one priority and work a lot like local chambers to offer business members credibility by referrals. Some groups, however, exist to increase memberships so the business group owner earns more membership fees. Other groups, thrive over turn over. Business goes to a few key members who have been around a long time and tend to be in insurance, real estate, or financial services. These groups count on member turn over to be introduced to new clients.

Once again, it pays to check for references from current and past members in your industry to determine whether membership will enhance your credibility. Ask about turn over before joining. Read the marketing material to see whether the group markets members or markets group membership. The bottom line about any group is whether or not your alliance provides you with more clients, access to better opportunities, or information that helps you grow your business that bring more money in than you spend to be a part of the group.

Bankers

People including bankers are more likely to make an extra effort on your behalf if they know and trust you. Build a relationship with a bank that has a reputation for doing business with small businesses such as yours.

Banks have target markets. If your business does $3 million a year in revenue and you chose a bank that targets businesses that do $10 million, you are in danger of being ignored. Some banks set aside funds for startups and others do not.

Ask if your banker will respond to e-mail requests from you. Before you sign, ask your banker if businesses such as yours are their target market. You can find out a lot by asking your banker who would be his or her best customer. The bank's focus should be congruent with your needs now. If you are a woman and/or you belong to a minority group, make sure the bank has a history of treating diverse groups and women equitably before opening your business account.

Even if the bank supports business owners such as you, the banker in front of you may not. If you are not the customer that most excites the banker in front of you ask to speak to someone who specializes in companies with your revenue and your needs. Do not be shy. They want your business. They should have to earn it.

Maintain your relationship. Occasionally, invite your banker to lunch or to an event. Good bankers love to network. They appreciate being introduced to possible customers as much as you do. If your banker does you a favor like releasing a large check for payment before the banks' standard waiting period, send a note, and say thank you. Connect with your banker on social media. Remember your banker's birthday. EVERYONE appreciates being remembered. EVERYONE gravitates consciously or subconsciously toward helping people they know to be thoughtful. Make sure your banker hears from you when you do not need help first.

In Conclusion

There is nothing more rewarding, frustrating, exhilarating, and exhausting than owning your own business. Become the business you would want to do business with now. Use best practices to build a business you are proud to own and operate. It may not happen overnight. Implementing best practices and earning to follow opportunity cycles takes time. If you feel overwhelmed then slow down but do not stop. If you did stop, there is no time like the present to start again. Take what you know and use it to build your business capacity fraction by fraction. Go forth and prosper.

Position List

Below is a general list of positions and the kind of work expected:

Employees—Employees are individual contributors who can have many titles such as specialists, technicians, administrative assistants, and so on.

Supervisors—Supervisors are in charge of the quality of work. They often schedule resources so that work planned can be successfully completed. They oversee production and make sure processes are followed.

Leads—A lead is a resource who offers guidance and direction to a small group of team members who have been tasked with achieving a goal or completing a project. The lead is often a more experienced team member who can provide instruction when asked. The job is to essentially lead the way to quality delivery making sure the correct processes are followed.

Managers—Managers are in charge of the information required to make sure the timing of work is always accurate. It is a common misconception that the main responsibility of a manager is to manage work. The most important duty of a manager is to move information in meetings and reports, and by providing status. Managers often use the information they know to create budgets for their department(s) or project(s) that become part of the larger budget as a whole. They oversee supervisors, propose, and manage processes, and work to resolve issues that impact smooth operations.

Directors—Directors do just what it sounds like they provide direction when overseeing their management teams. Directors make strategic recommendations. They own the budgets for their regions or department. Directors evaluate and may even be decision makers regarding key contracts. Directors help create and maintain company culture. They provide direction by making sure Managers and Supervisors are focused properly. They are responsible for raising the alarm and determining what needs to change when management teams are moving in the wrong direction to ensure all teams stay on track.

Vice Presidents—Vice Presidents are second-in-command for the company or for a single function. They sometimes run business segments or units for large companies that serve as an umbrella for several smaller ventures. Vice Presidents must be capable of stepping in if the CEO/President is suddenly unavailable. They usually have the authority to sign contracts. They may also be a signer on other legal documents. They approve and own the strategic plan built and implemented by directors and are responsible for making sure it stays in sync and on track.

Limited Liability Titles

The LLC structure is a membership structure and so C-Level executive titles do not quite fit. This structure is more flexible than a corporate structure. The same position may have a variety of titles.

Principal/Founder/Managing Partner/Owner/Consultant—These titles are all appropriate titles for the officers of an LLC. They are not only more flexible, but also less transparent. It may be harder to tell who the lead decision maker is just by an LLC title. Officers have an ownership interest in the company. Other employees do not. Officers are typically able to sign contracts, but those rights must be clearly outlined in the LLC founding documents. Some LLCs are fond of creatively naming positions to create a more egalitarian culture. Creative titles though can cause confusion for outsiders looking for the right person to contact.

Corporate Titles

C-Level executives—C-Level executives are part of a corporate structure. Sole proprietors and partnerships often use some of the same titles. These titles do not necessarily imply that an ownership interest in the company. There are a number of C-Level jobs in large corporate environments. Small businesses must be careful to use only titles they really need. The most common are:

CEO—Chief Executive Officer
CFO—Chief Financial Officer
CMO—Chief Marketing Officer
COO—Chief Operations Officer
CTO—Chief Technical Officer

Business Plan Outline

Executive Summary

About

    Mission

    Vision

    Values

    Leadership Team

History

Goals

Competitive Advantage

Financial Projections

Market

Pricing

Risks

Conclusion

Appendix

Growth Plan Outline

Access a template at CapacitySquared.net.
Executive Summary
About

    Mission
    Vision
    Values
    Founders

Advisory Board
History
Opportunity

    Revenue Streams
    KPIs
    Needs
    Challenges
    Solutions
    The Details

Market

    Market Strategies
    Customer Base
    Pricing
    Competitors

Risks
Organization
Financials
Conclusion
Appendix

Other Resources

- U.S. Gov Small Business Grants
  https://usagrantapplications.org/v9/?tc=ya&msclkid=57a474d
  4c7241a19dc8b2bb07f81b2fa
- Free SBA Business Page Next Door
  https://business.nextdoor.com/local/resources/announcing-
  business-posts-get-the-word-out-locally-about-your-
  business?utm_version=1&keyword= percent2Bsba.
  gov&matchtype=p&utm_term= percent2Bsba.gov&utm_
  campaign=targetingtype=nonbrand_smallbusinessadvertising_
  &utm_source=bing&utm_medium=paid_search&msclkid=
  89fff86ebac613173f1da70a011367e0

Accelerators

Information may change with no notice. See the updated list at CapacitySquared.net

Name	Benefactor	Contact
10,000 Small Businesses	Goldman Sachs/Babson College	Anyone can apply at www.10ksbapply.com/
Aspire	AT&T	Education-focused social entrepreneurs apply at https://about.att.com/csr/home/society/education/accelerator.html
Avanzar	Wells Fargo	Latino small business owners apply at https://prosperausa.org/avanzar-small-bussiness-accelerator-program/
Catapult	Capital One/ WBENC	Certified women-owned businesses apply at www.wbenc.org/blog-posts/2019/12/16/opportunities-open-doors-capital-one-catapult-program
Bunker Labs	Grants and Sponsorships	Veteran and veteran spouses apply at https://bunkerlabs.org/
Ground Floor	United Way	Social entrepreneurs may apply at https://unitedwayaccelerator.org/about/program-overview/
Target Accelerators	Target Forward Founders	Minority-owned early-stage product companies apply at https://target accelerators.com/programs/target-forward-founders/
Tori Burch Fellows	Tori Burch	Certified women-owned business apply at www.toryburchfoundation.org/about/
Unlocked Futures	Bank of America/Free America/New Profit	Formerly incarcerated social entrepreneurs apply at www.newprofit.org/go/eight-extraordinary-social-entrepreneurs-come-together-for-second-unlocked-futures-cohort/

Ancillaries

Find these templates, tools, and documents online at Capacity Squared.net

- Work Analysis Profile
- Link to Free Dominance, Influence, Steadiness and Compliance (DiSC) Personality Test
- Strengths, Weaknesses, Opportunities, Threats (SWOT) Map PDF to download
- Review of top-five SWOT mapping tools
- Operational Assessment
- Business Pan Template
- Growth Pan Template
- Review of top-ten process map tools
- Linear Process Map Template
- Swim Lane Process Map Template
- Review of top-ten most helpful small business sites
- Disaster Recovery Plan Template
- Various Business Best Practice Check Lists
- List of Accelerator/Incubator Programs
- List of Grant Opportunities

References

Association of Certified Fraud Examiners. 2020. "2020 Global Study on Occupational Fraud and Abuse." 5. https://acfepublic.s3-us-west-2.amazonaws .com/2020-Report-to-the-Nations.pdf (accessed November 15, 2021).

Bateman, A., A. Barrington, and K. Date. 2020. "Why You Need a Supplier-Diversity Program." *Harvard Business Review*, p. 4. Harvard University: Harvard Business Publishing.

Becker, R. 1991. *Anthropology Behind Defending the Caveman, R.* Performed by R. Becker. University of Texas at Dallas.

Bolton, R., and D.G. Bolton. 2009. *People Styles at Work and Beyond*, 2nd ed. New York, NY: Amacom.

Bourke, J. 2016. "How to Be Smarter and Make Better Choices. Directed by TEDxSouthBank." *Performed by J. Bourke.* www.youtube.com/watch?v=MZCy UANqYyw (accessed May 18, 2021).

Bourke, J. January 2018. "The Diversity and Inclusion Revolution: Eight Powerful Truths." *Deloitte Review.* www2.deloitte.com/us/en/insights/deloitte-review/ issue-22/diversity-and-inclusion-at-work-eight-powerful-truths.html?zd_ source=hrt&zd_campaign=53

Brinckmann, J., D. Grichnik, and D. Kapsa. 2017. "Should Entrepreneurs Plan or Just Storm the Castle? A Meta-Analysis on Contextual Factors Impacting the Business Planning–Performance Relationship in Small Firms." *Journal of Business Venturing*, no. 25, pp. 25–26. www.effectuation.org/ wp-content/uploads/2017/06/Should-entrepreneurs-plan-or-just-storm-the-castle_-A-meta-analysis-on-contextual-factors-impacting-the-business-planning%E2%80%93performance-relationship-in-small-firms-1.pdf

Burke, A.S., S. Fraser, and F.J. Greene. 2010. "The Multiple Effects of Business Planning on New Venture Performance." *Journal of Management Studies* 47, no. 3, pp. 391–415. Wiley-Blackwell Publishing Ltd. www.effectuation.org/ wp-content/uploads/2017/06/The-Multiple-Effects-of-Business-Planning-onNew-Venture-Performance-1.pdf

Capacity Squared. 2021. "About Us." https://capacitysquared.net/about/ (accessed November 24, 2021).

Corberly, C., 2021. "2021 Employee Engagement Report—People Element" http://PeopleElement-2021-Employee-Engagement-Report.pdf (accessed October 10, 2021).

Cox Business. 2020. *Cox Business #SBWSurvey.* Survey, Cox Business. www .coxblue.dreamhosters.com/wp-content/uploads/2013/06/infographic6_ sbwsurvey

Deloitte Global Human Capital. 2021. *2021 Delotte Global Human Capital Trends Survey.* Survey, Deloitte Insights, Deloitte, Inc. www2.deloitte.com/ us/en/insights/focus/human-capital-trends.html (accessed November 01, 2021).

Deloitte Inc. 2020. "The Deloitte Global Millennial Survey 2021." Survey, 18. www2.deloitte.com/global/en/pages/about-deloitte/articles/millennialsurvey .html

Deming, W.E. 1986. *Out of Crisis.* Massachusetts Institute of Technology, Center for Advanced Educational Services.

Deming, W.E., J. Orsini, and D.D. Cahill. 2012. *The Essential Deming: Leadership Principles from the Father of Quality.* McGraw-Hill Education.

Dixon-Fyle, S., V. Hunt, K. Dolan, and S. Prince. 2020. *Diversity Wins: How Inclusion Matters* 3. Survey, McKinsey and Company. Sundiatu Dixon-Fyle is a senior expert in McKinsey's London office, where Vivian Hunt, DBE, is a Senior Partner in McKinsey's London office. https://ucon.secure .nonprofitsoapbox.com/storage/diversity-wins-how-inclusion-matters-vf-2020.pdf (accessed August 22, 2021).

Dormann, C., PhD, and J. Gutenberg. November 2020. "Burnout Can Exacerbate Work Stress, Further Promoting A Vicious Circle." *Science Daily.* (accessed March 02, 2021).

Douglas, N. March 2007. "Next Big Thing Twitter blows up at SXSW Conference." www.gawker.com/243634/twitter-blows-up-at-sxsw-conference (accessed June 07, 2021).

Ferry, K. 2021. "Korn Ferry 2021 Buyes Preferences Study, Reconnecting with Buyers." *Study* 13. https://infokf.kornferry.com/rs/494-VUC-482/images/ Korn_Ferry_2021_Buyer_Preferences_Study.pdf

Fung, K. May 2021. "Shopify CEO Sends Email to Staff Saying Company Is 'Not a Family'." *Newsweek,* 159. www.newsweek.com/shopify-ceo-sends-email-staff-saying-company-not-family-we-cannot-solve-every-societal-159

George, B., R.M. Walker, and J. Monster. 2019. "Does Strategic Planning Improve Organizational Performance? A Meta-Analysis." *Public Administration Review (PAR)* 79, no. 6, pp. 810–819. https://doi.org/10.1111/puar.13104 2019 (accessed February 12, 2021).

Greene, P. PhD interview by S. Hardin. July 17, 2021. *Founder of the Diana Project and former Director of the Women's Bureau of the U.S. Department of Labor.*

Greene, P., interview by S. Hardin. July 17, 2021. *Founder of the Diana Project and Former Director of the Women's Bureau of the U.S. Department of Labor.*

Hantula, D. 1995. "Disciplined Decision Making in an Interdisciplinary Environment." *The Journal of Applied Behavior Analysis* 28, no. 3, pp. 371–377. https://onlinelibrary.wiley.com/toc/19383703/1995/28/3

Hardin, S. January 05, 2021. "Capacity Squared Mission." https://capacity squared.net/about/ (accessed January 05, 2021).

Humphreys, J. 2003. "The Dysfunctional Evolution of Goal Setting." *MIT Sloan Management Review* 44, no. 4, p. 96. Massachusetts Institute of Technology. https://sloanreview.mit.edu/article/the-dysfunctional-evolution-of-goal-setting-2/

IRS. 2021. "Independent Contractor Defined." *IRS.* www.irs.gov/businesses/small-businesses-self-employed/independent-contractor-defined (accessed August 03, 2021).

Kaplan, S., and A.B. Tran. 2021. "Nearly 1 in 3 Americans Experienced a Weather Disaster This Summer." *Washington Post* 1. www.washingtonpost .com/climate-environment/2021/09/04/climate-disaster-hurricane-ida/

Locke, E., and G. Latham. 2013. *New Developments in Goal Setting and Task Performance.* Walsworth Publishing Company.

Mann, M. 2015. "How a Five Letter Word Built a 104 Year Old Company." *Smithsonian Magazine.* www.smithsonianmag.com/smithsonian-institution/how-five-letter-word-built-104-year-old-company-180955899/

Moskovitz, D. 2021. *Your Mission is Our Mission.* https://blog.asana .com/2020/09/mission/ (accessed November 29, 2021).

Mrazek, D., interview by S. Hardin. September 29, 2021. *Founder of the Sales Company and Marketing Adjunct Faculty 10,000 Small Businesses.*

Murray, M. 2019. "The Balance Small Business." *The Balance.* www.thebalancesmb .com/federal-express-fedex-2221098 (accessed September 08, 2021).

Nike. 2021. *Breaking Barriers.* https://purpose.nike.com/ (accessed November 24, 2021).

O'Neill, L., interview by S. Hardin. August 09, 2021. *CEO O'Neill Enterprises and Lead Faculty and Facilitator for 10,000 Small Businesses.*

Oswald, A., PhD., E. Proto, PhD., and D. Sgroi, PhD. 2015. *Happiness and Productivity. JSTOR Collection* 33, no. 4, 790. University of Chicago: The University of Chicago Press.

Park, M.Y. September 2013. "A History of the Cake Mix, the Invention That Redefined 'Baking." *Bon Appetit.* www.bonappetit.com/entertaining-style/pop-culture/article/cake-mix-history

Poll, H. 2020. "Diversity & Inclusion Workplace Survey." 1–5. Glassdoor. www .glassdoor.com/employers/blog/diversity-inclusion-workplace-survey/

Purvin, D., interview by S. Hardin. October 26, 2021. *Senior Vice President at a National Bank and Founder of the Business Owner's MBA.*

Reid, D. October 20, 2021. *Saes Director.*

Renjen, P. 2021. *2021 Deloitte Global Resilience Report, Building the resilient organization,* pp. 3–4. Annual Report, Deloitte Inc. www2.deloitte .com/content/dam/insights/articles/US114083_Global-resilience-and-disruption/2021-Resilience-Report.pdf (accessed November, 2021).

Rosenberg, M.B. 2003. *Nonviolent Communication: A Language of Life,* 2nd ed. Encinitas: Puddledancer Press.

SBA. 2019. "Federal Government Achieves Small Business Contracting Goal for Sixth Consecutive Year with Record-Breaking $120 Billion to Small Businesses." Release Number: 19–36, SBA. www.sba.gov/about-sba/sba-newsroom/press-releases-media-advisories/federal-government-achieves-small-business-contracting-goal-sixth-consecutive-year-record-breaking

SBA. 2021. "United States Small Business Profile." Government, Office of Small Business Advocacy. https://cdn.advocacy.sba.gov/wp-content/uploads/2021/08/30143723/Small-Business-Economic-Profile-US.pdf

SBA. n.d. "Small Business Administration, Office of Advocacy." https://cdn .advocacy.sba.gov/wp-content/uploads/2020/06/04144224/2020-Small-Business-Economic-Profile-US.pdf (accessed October 15, 2021).

Schopenhauer, A. 2010. *The Essential Schopenhauer: Key Selections from The World As Will and Representation and Other Writings.* New York, NY: Harper Perennial Modern Thought.

Schwarzkopf, S., and R. Gries. 2010. *Ernest Dichter and Motivation Research: New Perspectives on the Making of Post-war Consumer Culture.* New York, NY: Palgrave Macmillan.

Shankland, S. June 2004. "IBM Regains Super Computer Bragging Rights." www.techrepublic.com/article/ibm-regains-supercomputer-bragging-rights/ (accessed February 19, 2021).

Starbucks. 2021. "Starbucks." www.starbucks.com/careers/working-at-starbucks/ culture-and-values (accessed May 10, 2021).

Strader, A., interview by S. Hardin. October 10, 2021. *Former Military Hostage Negotiator and Small Business Owner.*

Sull, D., and C. Sull. 2021. "10 Things Your Culture Needs to Get Right." *MIT Sloan.* Massachusetts Institute of Technology.

Sull, D., and C. Sull. September 16, 2021. "10 Things Your Corporate Culture Needs to Get Right." *MIT Sloan Management Review.* MIT SMR/Glassdoor Culture 500. https://sloanreview.mit.edu/article/10-things-your-corporate-culture-needs-to-get-right/

Sun Trust Team. 2017. "Sun Trust Team, Piling up Profits Five Best Practices to Increase your Business's Profitability." Corporate Report, 4. www.suntrust .com/content/dam/suntrust/us/en/small-business/2017/documents/best-practice-guide-increase-profitability.pdf

Tesla. 2021. "About Tesla." www.tesla.com/about (accessed November 24, 2021).

Tinsley, C., PhD., and E.T. Amanatulla. 2012. "Punishing Female Negotiators for Asserting Too Much…Or not Enough: Exploring Why Advocacy Moderates Backlash Against Assertive Female Negotiators." *Organization Behavior and Human Decision Processes,* pp. 110–122. Elsevier. www.academia .edu/57788090/Punishing_female_negotiators_for_asserting_too_much_ or_not_enough_Exploring_why_advocacy_moderates_backlash_against_ assertive_female_negotiators (accessed July 12, 2021).

Training Magazine. November/December 2020. "2020 Training Industry Report." November/December: 23. https://pubs.royle.com/publication/ ?m=20617&i=678873&p=24.

Tseng, J., and J. Poppenk. 2020. "Brain Meta-State Transitions Demarcate Thoughts Across Task Contexts Exposing the Mental Noise of Trait Neuroticism." *National Column* 11, no. 3480, p. 3480. https://doi.org/ 10.1038/s41467-020-17255-9

Turner, A. 2018. *Capitalism in the Age of Robots: Work, Income and Wealth in the 21st-Century.* You Tube. Produced by Global Commission Collection, Institute of New Economic Thinking, Performed by A. Turner. https://youtu. be/D6FBL6c6C5E (accessed September 01, 2021).

U.S. Bureau of Labor Statistics. n.d. "Consumer Price Index." *Economic News Release* 1. www.bls.gov/news.release/cpi.nr0.htm (accessed November 23, 2021).

U.S. Chamber of Commerce. 2021. "45 Grants, Loans and Programs to Benefit Your Small Business." www.uschamber.com/co/run/business-financing/ government-small-business-grant-programs?utm_medium=Email&utm_ source=SFMC&utm_campaign=MO_Newsletter&utm_content=2021_ 06_03 (accessed August 03, 2021).

Yli-Renko, H., L. Denoo, and R. Janakiraman. 2020. "A Knowledge-Based View of Managing Dependence on a Key Customer: Survival and Growth Outcomes for Young Firms." *Journal of Business Venturing* 35, no. 6. Elsevier.

About the Author

Sheryl Hardin is an author and speaker with a passion for Organizational Change Management (OCM) and continuous process improvement. She is also an entrepreneur and Cofounder of Capacity Squared (C2). She enjoys assisting companies as they create a business strategy, manage change, prepare for rapid growth, govern strategic projects, and improve processes. She can often be found speaking and consulting as a national speaker, seminar leader, adjunct faculty instructor, and business advisor. Sheryl uses carefully planned operational analysis and process improvement strategies that inspire organizational best practices.

Sheryl focuses on quelling the chaos that comes from infrastructures that are not properly sized to support an organization and operations that do not support best practices. Her special skill is finding the pieces of the puzzle that support rapid change while consulting with companies in a wide variety of industries. Her writing is inspired by real business experience that includes organization-impacting activities that guide success.

Index

accelerators, 44–45, 239
accountability, 190–191, 222–224
accounts payable (AP), 227
accounts receivable (AR), 227
acquire disrupters, 74
acquisitions, 45–49
action items, 217
action plan, 107
adjust three key constraints, 127–128
advisory board, 229
age, 68
agenda, 216
agile status meetings, 34–35
aging, 227
align, 61–62
ancillaries, 241
Angel Investors, 116
Annual Revenue Per User (ARPU), 125, 126
artificial intelligence (AI), 196–197
Asana, 20
assess, 59–60
asset, 38–39
audience focused instructions, 140–141
audits, 209–213
automation, 195–197

balance sheet, 123
bankers, 231–232
barriers, 85
barter, 128
Becker, R., 201–202
Being Bankable, 118–119
Bezos, J., 104
book value, 228, 229
Bourke, J., 179
break even, 227
brief instructions, 141–142
budget, 108, 125
build, lease, and buy, 128
burnout, 177–183

business
  baseline, 79
  education programs, 44–45
  plan, 77–78, 236
  story, 79
  structure, 131–132
Business-to-Business (B2B), 64
Business-to-Consumer (B2C), 64
Business-to-Government (B2G), 64
buyer evaluation, 64–65
buyer research, 97–100

capacity, 1, 25–26, 119
CapacitySquared (C2), 20, 23, 115, 193
capital, 120
cash flow, 122, 227
cash on hand, 122, 227
chambers, 230–231
change, 159–162
  communication, 165
  and culture, 200–206
  goals, 163
  job responsibilities, 180
  KPIs, 163–164
  milestones, 165
  operational capacity, 183–200
  opportunities for, 180–181
  and pivots, 42
  reinforcement, 166
  resistance, 164
  review, 162–163
  SMEs, 164
  stakeholders, 164
  team management, 166–176
channels, 83–87
  identification, 88–90
  paths, 90
  testing, 90–95
character, 120–121
chatting, 155–156
checklists, 194

churn rate, 125
civil emergencies, 199
clear instructions, 143
clear leader, 216
C-Level executives, 235
Coberly, C., 221
collaboration, 156, 204–205
collateral, 120
communication, 165
company values, 19
competitive
    advantage, 209
    edge, 73
    pricing, 100–101
competitors
    evaluation, 71–72, 75–77
    metrics, 73
    mistakes, 73
conditions, 121
confidence, 171
constant process improvement, 159,
        172, 189–190, 214–215
contractor, 39–40
cost of goods sold (COGS), 228
cost of success, 79
cost plus pricing, 101
Cox Business, 16
credibility, 41, 187–189
credit history, 226
creditworthy, 225
cross-functional maps, 135–136
crowd funding, 113
Cuban, M., 204
culture, 11–13
    change and, 200–206
    contamination, 36–37
    quiz, 11–13
customer base, 96–97
Customer Relationship Management
        (CRM), 96
customer/user experience, 91

dashboards, 219–220
data universal numbering system
        (DUNS), 188
Davis, B., 211
deadlines, 157, 224
decision points, 171
decisions, 85

delegation process, 172–175
delivery, 9
Deloitte Global Human Capital
        Trends survey, 1–2, 11
Deloitte Global Millennial Survey
        2020, 176
demand-based pricing, 101–102
Deming, W. E., 160–161, 191
designing, 130–131
design phase, 129
detailed map, 136–137
development phase, 145–146
Dichter, E., 92
digital footprint, 73–74
directors, 233
disaster recovery plan, 213–214
discount equipment acquisition, 47
disruptions, 9
diversity, equity, and inclusion (DEI),
        45
documentation, 133–134, 165,
        189–193
document issues, 217
Dormann, C., 177
due diligence, 48–49
Dunn and Bradstreet, 188

earnings, 228
earnings before interest and taxes
        (EBIT), 228
earnings before interest, taxes,
        depreciation, and
        amortizations (EBITDA),
        124, 228
earnings before taxes (EBT), 124, 228
education, 68
effective
    meetings, 215–218
    procedure checklist, 144
    process checklist, 139
efficient and effective instructions,
        143
Eisenhower Matrix, 206
Electronic Data Systems (EDS), 35
elevator pitch tease, 110–112
employees, 39–40, 233
end goal, 21–23
equipment, 132–133
    leases, 117

evaluation, 62–77
events, 94–95
execution phase
    design and prep, 129–133
    develop, 145–146
    document, 133–144
executive suite, 40–41
expectations, 172
experimentation, 94
experts, 170
exposure, 108

failure threat, 37–38
fake experts, 169
familiarity, 97–98
financial, 224–229
    audits, 210–211
    issues, 8
    reports, 221–222
    software, 185–186, 225
five Cs of credit, 119–121
flexibility, 205
focus groups, 91–94
follow-up, 218, 224
forecasts, 125
formatting, 193–194
forms, 194
fractional leaders, 40–41,
    168–170
franchise, 188
frequently asked questions (FAQ),
    195
full-time, 40
fund, 112–128

gaps, 74, 191–192
gender, 69
Generally Accepted Accounting
    Principles (GAAP), 49, 210
geographical region, 97
George, B., 28
Glassdoor D&I (Diversity and
    Inclusion) Workplace Survey
    (2020), 37
good plan, 78–80
government contracting, 44
government grants, 114
grants, 114–115
Greene, P., 15, 16, 225

gross profit margin, 228
growing capacity, 43–49
growth plan, 78, 237

habits, 69
Hantula, D., 131
Harvard Business Review, 45
help, 226
high-level strategies, 79
hiring, 167–168
    fractional leaders and experts,
        168–172
    resources, 168
history, 5–6
honesty, 203
Hopper, G., 98

IBM, 98
impersonators, 169
implementation phase
    implement, 149–150
    quality assurance, 146–148
    train and support, 148–149
implementation plan, 149–150
income, 69
    statement, 123–124
Initial Public Offering (IPO), 22
initiation phase, 58
    align, 61–62
    assess, 59–60
    evaluate, 62–77
    opportunity, 58–59
insurance, 229–232
integrity, 203
intelligent questions, 170–171
interest investors, 72
Internal Revenue Service (IRS),
    167–168
International Organization for
    Standardization (ISO), 224
investors, 188–189
    funding, 115–117

job descriptions, 166–167
Just In Time (JIT), 191

Kaplan, S., 213
Key Performance Indicators (KPIs),
    29

Korn Ferry, 67
KPIs, 163–164, 184–185

Latham, G., 163
lawsuits, 10
leadership, 42
leads, 233
legality, 61–62
LLC title, 234
loans, 117–119
location, 70–71
Locke, E., 163
longevity, 187
loyalty, 86

McDonalds, 188
management periods, 34
managers, 233
market/marketing, 26
    campaigns, 95–96
    changes, 73, 197–200
    channel options, 89
    evaluation, 63–64
    saturation, 64
    share expansion, 46
    strategy, 83–100
match, 66
meeting notes, 217
mergers, 45–49
metrics, 79, 184–185
milestone checkpoints, 33
milestones, 165
mismatch, 38
mission, 19–20
mixed pricing, 102
Monster, J., 28
Monthly Recurring Revenue (MRR), 125–126
motivation, 16–18, 176
Mrazek, D., 107
multiple sales, 106

national registration programs, 45
net earnings, 124
net profit margin, 228
networking groups, 231
net worth, 228
new innovations, 199
new perspectives, 42

niche opportunities, 198–199
Nike, 23
nonprofit, 115
numbered instructions, 142–143

O'Neill, L., 167
one sale, 106
online communities, 230
online reviews, 9
on time payments, 226
operating cash flow, 227
operational
    assessment, 27–28
    audits, 211
    budgets, 186–187
    capacity, 183–200
    dashboards, 219–220
opportunity, 26, 73
    for innovation, 180–181
    statement, 58–59
Opportunity Development Life
    Cycle (ODLC), 55–57;
        See also execution phase;
        implementation phase;
        initiation phase; plan phase;
        review phase
organizational chart, 42–43
Oswald, A., 11
Otis, E., 110
outside funding, 113–119
owners' draw, 228
owners'/shareholders' equity, 228, 229

Park, M. Y., 92
partner, 128
partnership, 189
part-time, 40
passive ownership, 21–22
patterns, 86
penetration, 98
people threat, 37
Perot, R., 35
personality testing, 178–179
planning reviews, 33–34
plan phase
    fund, 112–128
    plan, 77–80
    strategize, 80–112
point of pain/inconvenience, 65

policies and procedures, 222–223
position list, 233
positive change, 192
practical plans, 171
preparation, 131
pre-seed, 115
pricing assumptions, 74
pricing strategy, 100–102
priorities, 70, 87
prioritize development, 74
priority setting, 206
private grants, 114
process improvement, 214–215
process map, 134–139
Product Development Life Cycle
    (PLC), 52–53
pro forma, 49
project audits, 211–212
Project Development Life Cycle
    (PDLC), 53–54
Proto, E., 11
prototype, 143–144
purpose driven instructions, 140
Purvin, D., 118

quality assurance, 146–148

refinements, 108
registration, 45
regulatory changes, 199–200
Reid, D., 1
reinforcement, 166
Renjen, P., 159
reports, 194, 218–222
reputation, 6–10
reputation checklist, 7
Requests for Proposals (RFPs), 208
requirements checklist, 129–130
reserves, 122
resistance management, 164
resources, 106–107
respect, 202–203
return on investment (ROI), 228
review maps, 138–139
review phase, 150–151
risks, 15–16, 80, 190
    assessments, 209
    management, 207–214
    register, 209
roadmap to success, 29–33, 78, 82, 206

safe confession, 222
safe instructions, 142
safety audit, 212–213
sales
    funnels, 104–106
    goals, 104
    meeting agenda, 109–110
    meetings, 108–109
    pitch, 109–112
    plan, 103–104
    processes, 107–109
    reports, 221
    strategy, 103–104
scalability, 42
scaling up, 47
seed, 116
selling, 22
Series A, 116
Series B, 116
Series C, 116–117
Sgroi, D., 11
short meetings, 217–218
simple instructions, 140
simple map, 134–135
Small Business Administration (SBA),
    1, 8, 15, 16, 44, 143, 159, 226
Special Purpose Acquisition Company
    (SPAC), 116
stability, 98–99
stakeholders, 164
Standard Operating Procedures
    (SOPs), 139
standards, 223–224
Starbucks, 20
start and end on time, 216–217
starting today, 18–24
startups, 72
stated purpose, 216
status reports, 157–158, 220–221
strategic goals, 81–82
strategic planning, 28–35
strategize, 80–112
Subject Matter Expert (SME), 164
success, 172–175
Sull, C., 200, 202
Sull, D., 200, 202
supervisors, 233
supply chain flexibility, 47–48
support, 165, 184
    groups, 230

Swim Lanes. *See* cross-functional maps
SWOT analysis, 208
System Development Life Cycle (SDLC), 54–55
system level maps, 138, 139

team management, 166–176
teams, 35–43
templates, 193–195
termination, 182–183
Tesla, 23
time, 174
timelines, 80
time management, 205–206
time strategy, 82
Tinsley, C., 10
top-down maps, 137
tough negotiations, 10
tracking, 108
training, 148–149, 165, 177
Training Industry Report (2020), 177
Tran, A. B., 213

transparency, 204
trends, 198
Turner, A., 195
turnover, 179–181

values, 69–70, 99–100, 192–193
venture capitalists (VCs), 116, 192–193
verbal warning, 182
Vice Presidents, 233
vision, 23–24
visual instructions, 141
volume, 99

Walker, R., 28
wants, 70
Watson, T. Jr., 98
website, 187
WordPerfect, 91
workflow diagrams, 137–138
working capital, 229
written warning, 182, 183

year end income, 124–125

OTHER TITLES IN THE ENTREPRENEURSHIP AND SMALL BUSINESS MANAGEMENT COLLECTION

Scott Shane, Case Western University, Editor

- *The Startup Master Plan* by Nikhil Agarwal and Krishiv Agarwal
- *Managing Health and Safety in a Small Business* by Jacqueline Jeynes
- *Modern Devil's Advocacy* by Robert Koshinskie
- *Dead Fish Don't Swim Upstream* by Silverberg Jay
- *The 8 Superpowers of Successful Entrepreneurs* by Marina Nicholas
- *Founders, Freelancers & Rebels* by Helen Jane Campbell
- *Time Management for Unicorns* by Giulio D'Agostino
- *Zero to $10 Million* by Shane Brett
- *Navigating the New Normal* by Rodd Mann
- *Ethical Business Culture* by Andreas Karaoulanis
- *Blockchain Value* by Olga V. Mack
- *TAP Into Your Potential* by Rick De La Guardia
- *Stop, Change, Grow* by Michael Carter and Karl Shaikh
- *Dynastic Planning* by Walid S. Chiniara

Concise and Applied Business Books

The Collection listed above is one of 30 business subject collections that Business Expert Press has grown to make BEP a premiere publisher of print and digital books. Our concise and applied books are for...

- Professionals and Practitioners
- Faculty who adopt our books for courses
- Librarians who know that BEP's Digital Libraries are a unique way to offer students ebooks to download, not restricted with any digital rights management
- Executive Training Course Leaders
- Business Seminar Organizers

Business Expert Press books are for anyone who needs to dig deeper on business ideas, goals, and solutions to everyday problems. Whether one print book, one ebook, or buying a digital library of 110 ebooks, we remain the affordable and smart way to be business smart. For more information, please visit www.businessexpertpress.com, or contact sales@businessexpertpress.com.

CPSIA information can be obtained
at www.ICGtesting.com
Printed in the USA
JSHW042253180922
30345JS00001B/10